Bright and

(The Anarchi

An Attempt To Build On Machiavelli's Discourses, Themselves Built On The Wisdom Of The Ancient Greek Philosophies

Michael Heeneman

Contents

To my family and friends, I would not be here without you.

Synopsis

This book sets about relating our politics within the biological framework within which it exists. We are biological beings and our systems need to relate to this. The book is grounded in the belief that these systems should work for us both as individuals and as a collective. We also cover maths, markets, our instinctive chimpanzee troop nature , a little on war, population control and melding. The title gives away my feeling that Machiavelli needed updating, rulers once did not have to be too accountable but with education now we are all to a degree political princes if we want to be. Many of us though do not want all power with the government rather the people. I call these people Anarchist Princes. All of us who wish to can now hold politicians to account, feed ideas to them and get involved in a variety of ways. This book ultimately seeks to grab all of these strands and put them in a form that is digestible.

Foreword

This book is the result of experience, learning and exasperation. My tribe once was Goth with all the anarchic ideals it held, but whilst their arguments have developed on from my time in that tribe I find it hard to see how their politics have changed much in the outside world. I feel that there will always be a traditional and contemporary part of society but as communication has changed in the physical, electronic sense of the word, instead of contemporary groupings uniting over issues, they just splinter into smaller and smaller (and so weaker) non communicating groups who can unite on what they disagree with, but alas not nearly so much with what they agree with when it comes to the devil in the detail.

This book is (optimistically?) aimed as a help to anyone wishing to grapple the contradictions of politics in relation to life outside it, whether they just want to understand, or take the plunge, risk unpopularity and do.

All my best wishes to anyone who tries, but remember no one is the perfect anarchist prince(ss), and sexual generality is assumed and sometimes used from here. An anarchist leaves control to others, a prince seeks control themselves, we balance somewhere between as individual human beings. However an anarchist prince in the context of this book will see both poles at work and the fact that we cannot bind fully to one or another, as all people are different. The aim of this book is to use biological structures to take account of both.

Mike.

Chapter 1: Whatever you do stay within the system.

This chapter aims to focus all thoughts in the further chapters to be within the system, and to recognise the need for systematic control despite its drawbacks. N.B. The Nelson Mandela test comes later on at the end of the book as a balance to this chapter.

Political Control and Reform

Although we may feel that we can change everything, we are defined in no small part by the system and belief systems in which we are reared. We needed the systems of parental care and guidance, language, friends, their parents, societal norms and conflicts around them to develop an , even if only initial, direction that will shape many of our moves.

A plot of land without political control which is also known as a place with a power vacuum leads to groups seeking to assert it and very quickly disintegrates into violence, even if things integrate after. The reason for this is clear, if everyone was to change just their jobs, let alone their dwellings, by lottery, people would turn up to work the next day untrained and by lottery most likely without anyone to train them. Even if a number knew what to do, many would still not know how to do it and an obvious implication of this is that food supplies would not distribute with the resulting hunger. Food shortages occur every Christmas, somewhere in Britain there is traditionally a fight over the last Turkey in a supermarket, even when there are other meats available.

The alternative to ripping up all current control in other words a revolution is to build on what exists which is not necessarily acceptance of the system, rather a reformers attitude: there are parts of any system that are beneficial, for example a legal system, if not individual laws, or we would not accept it as a whole and it is the beneficial parts that need building on with the other parts needing reforming.

Evolution frames Revolution

Evolution is how we biologically came to be, and in a different way has developed most of our legal systems. Evolution can be comparatively slow like the growth of animals generation by generation naturally or more quickly by selective breeding. A large asteroid hitting the earth with all of the resulting extinctions would be a revolution but the resulting evolution is still slow. Russia had a revolution in 1917 and many aspects of the old system were quickly dismantled, but the work on the economy still needed time to develop. Similarly with our systems, we can build and reform them over long periods. Education has been around for and has changed over tens of thousands of years, or looking at it from a non humanist view since we were monkeys, lemurs or before. An environmental change, like the effective asteroid of the banking collapse in 2008, precipitates major changes in shorter spaces of time, normally seen as radical or revolutionary, yet those changes will also get honed over time pulling them into the frame of human evolution as the resulting restrictions on banks will grow and show. Therefore any form of revolutionary attitude historically in the fullness of time will be as a part of either disaster or development and evolution. Communism in Russia was seen as slow progress, Communism with the Khmer Rouge in Cambodia was seen as genocide. At the time of writing the controls are still being placed over banks but the virtuosity of these reforms have yet to be seen, let alone be built on. They will either be beneficial or the system will likely collapse again within 20 or so years.

Legal Systems and Corruption

One of the greatest problems with progress is that it is incremental. New is built on old, which in turn often was built on something older. If a given law is not precise in application many grievances will arise and ultimately the law will either be overturned for example the UK Community Charge(Poll Tax) or updated (Criminal Justice sentencing policy for a given crime being an obvious candidate). A legal system has to have the sanctions to make people fear it, but the clarity and fairness for people not to rise up against it. People are happy to fear the law, they are not happy to live in fear of the law.

A major problem with any legal system is that it needs to be presumed at large as 'good' and will protect its name as such and if necessary protect the corrupt as their discovery can undermine the system. This need to appear as 'good' applies to all areas operating within the legal system, from government (the law makers), the police who risk their lives to protect the law (law givers), companies, who spend fortunes on lawyers to hide malpractice, traditionally charities and certainly local councils. Working within a system is no protection from the corrupt (who will call you corrupt and lie to prove it), but failing to work within it allows those same people to accuse the individual of undermining the system itself. It is better to be called corrupt within the system than to be accused of trying to destroy it because the former is expected of politicians (anarchist prince or not) and the latter risks all in the system uniting against you, which is futile unless you are genuinely trying to bring down the system.

The balance that an anarchist prince needs to strike is to progress the system at a pace whereby vested interests being lost are not lost at a rate as to make the corrupt overly fear for their downfall or ways of old. If the corrupt do overly fear, it is in their interests to try to link their downfall with the destruction of the system or ways that they assert the system must embrace. Indeed, the anarchist prince will do well also to know that when the corrupt cannot destroy an argument that goes against their interests, they will turn on the agent of that argument. At that stage, the more an argument can be made to be seen as to threaten the system, then the more they have license to destroy the agent of that argument personally. However, the more the changes proposed are seen as part of progress, the less the corrupt will be able to manoeuvre.

Chapter 2: You do not need any credit, but must risk danger.

The aim of this chapter is to get the reader to realise how they often need to let go of glory to the fraternity of politicians to get ideas up, but will still risk immense danger if they effect any true change.

Politicians talk and the ideas are theirs

Who initiated the NHS? Labour? Attlee? Bevan? Beveridge? The Brains Trust[1]? None of the above, yet all played a part. But if the Brains Trust came up with the idea, it is likely that either one person or a group in conversation that came up with the idea but got no credit. It would not bother them, nor should it, they were interested in the health of others, but for all their merits, no politicians were interested in giving them credit. This represents both a strength and a weakness for someone aspiring to affect policy: The weakness is to risk no credit, which is fine if you lose little, but if you lose much you earn contempt for not having got anything out for yourself, merely others or worse still just getting credit for the politicians who get the glory yet are rarely seen as being much help. The strength of giving away your ideas is that by offering the credit to the self interest of politicians it makes it a sweetener for them to put in the effort to make the idea(s) policy. A politician's greatest dream is to be remembered in 10,000 years time, the anarchist prince wishing to increase their chances of helping their fellow citizens must help the politician in that dream of glory but not compete with it, such is the vanity of rulers.

Politicians crave the power that they think solves everything

Of course by helping one politician in their vanities, you take away from others. Unfortunately politicians do not like consensus, rather the glory for themselves, and the ones who feel left out still have power. Civil Servants, Doctors, Police, Teachers all fear this power. Indeed political parties are also very capable of character assassination, groupings of thousands of people can propagate lies in a way that no individual can counter, thus lowering that individual's position to the point where many are incentivised to abuse their powers to make these self fulfilling prophesies. It is seen as acceptable to abuse people once they are branded a fool, or fools. All genocides require a people to be talked down first, most violence towards an individual requires exactly the same.

To give ideas to one politician endangers you from others and some will try to destroy you. It must be remembered that to a politician, power and position are more important than virtue or truth, especially if they are already power corrupted. They will always point to exceptions like Wilberforce but he was ganged up on for years by other politicians (vested interests) to the point of needing a bodyguard[2] after making his principled stand on slavery, proving that standard politicians have no right to claim those few as of their own. Their desire for position and power is no substitute for subtle imaginative policy.

A totally power corrupted Hitler wrecked millions in his rampage. The European politicians' solution is not subtle, rather to concentrate power even more and have a head of state in a new country called Europe with a federal dream of that person having even more power than Hitler. This shows that politicians instinctively want power to themselves; they see power as a solution for extreme problems, when the extremes of power normally cause these problems. Many politicians objectify power to themselves as a solution, indicating a lack of understanding of the separation and so delegation of power. Oddly they have normally been taught about the separation of power before they make laws in governments, but seem to forget about that once they have some power for themselves.

People who bow to power too easily are the most likely to take part in tyranny

Apart from the obvious, it should also be noted that people normally treat others as they wish to be treated themselves. Politicians can be very respectful or they can have graces or some blend of both. If they bow too much to their bosses, they expect people to bow too much to them. These people take orders and expect those underneath to accept that, whatever the order. The start of tyranny is flattery because flattery starts within the self and these people flatter their bosses to such an extent that no morality will stop them from doing as they are told.

Grasping of power and the risk of jealousy

When any individual is seen to have influence or power within one party, the other party will accept this if they think that person has no virtuosity. If they think they are virtuous they will fear their work and seek to remove them from that position. This happened in the 1997 Labour administration where Alistair Campbell, Tony Blair's Press Secretary was quickly seen as the top target for The Conservatives[3]. He had the protection of his boss, the Prime Minister and it took a total of six years to remove him. An anarchist prince need expect no such protection from any criticism or corruption: As the prime minister's press secretary, Campbell's job was to sell the party and so hide corruption. An anarchist prince will cause division by trying to change a party and so many peoples' vested interests. The anarchist prince will also note that those corrupted even if only in their fears about those interests will work together across party lines united in fear. This is not surprising, in the case of national interest, the parties can come legitimately together, and in politics if the cause is not legitimate, that doesn't stop people coming together anyway.

The dangers of politicians, power, life and existentialism

People are fickle and are interested in their own affairs. They do understand someone doing something for no great gain provided that person suffers no great loss. If a person suffers great loss people's instincts for their own affairs lead to contempt for that person not managing theirs. Power which politicians hold can give them the capacity to leave people in such dire situations that what started out with no great loss ends up with an enormous one. This mechanism is a way for politicians to destroy ideas, facts and people that find them when they are inconvenient and politicians can use this to terrify others into submission.

An inconvenient voice is the 1930s was a UK backbench MP who was extremely worried about Hitler. He was hated by groupings that wanted to deal with Hitler who felt their financial and positional domestic interests were safer with him than with redistributing wealth around the nation which was the up and coming political agenda from the left. He was alone, despised and talked existentially down by his own party and was to call the period the ten most lonely years of his life. He would later lead that party to its greatest victory in 1945, against the very Hitler that most of his party had supported. That was major personal destruction followed by ultimate victory, it turned his opponents in his party to his greatest fans.

However, a capital example of this fear of power is the UK government's likely murder of Dr Kelly in 2003[4] Where now the evidence is being kept under lock and key for up to 70 years[5] when he had evidence the government had lied to take our country to war, this is unlikely to be proven, corruption saw to that scientist being accused of 'losing the plot,' questioning his stability (and implicitly his work) existentially and then ultimately by taking his life. No one else spoke out about Weapons of Mass Destruction in Iraq after this, fear had silenced them as the government had shown they were willing to kill their own in their determination to kill others in a war as controversial as any since the second world war.

Ultimately, whatever the engagements over party differences, politicians are a fraternity and not confident enough in their judgement in the main to be able to contemplate life without people fearing them, that is why 'the other side' rarely bother to chase conspiracies when they come to power, it is a done deal based on keeping position over the people. They are in it together and the anarchist prince should beware power, his or her name and physical safety if they wish to effect change that takes power from the powerful. Even if some of the powerful do agree with you, they cannot support you fully, as they have fraternity to hold.

Chapter 3: The Party that is harder to persuade will provide ultimate victory.

This chapter aims to make clear that you need to win over the unconverted far more than the converted.

All Parties need to be involved.

In the context of Western Democracy traditions arise within parties when the policy of two leaders in power uphold a new principle but become national traditions when the main parties finally agree on a space for a national concept to sustain in. Once again this is because more than one leader agrees, under Machiavelli's conclusions.

This concept can be a constitutional, legal or administrative mechanism, or an attitude leading to a change in language, mindset. Arguments move like pendulum arcs which slowly damp to a balance. All parties have a part to play in the development of a policy, both proposition and opposition, pro or against.

The Party that is easiest to please loses as easily as it is pleased.

The party that is easiest to please with a set of thoughts that aspire to national concept is also the party whose members are most likely to get over excited. People want politicians to provide extravagant bells and whistles with all of their work, but few would accept the cost if that were the case.

The problem with a group of people overly enthusing about something is that because their hearts are flowing with joy, they immediately assume that other hearts will also, which is not necessarily correct. In this state people are likely to add detail or principle that may be aesthetically pleasing but costs (socially, financially, in relation to liberty) heavily and so makes their policy cumbersome to an extent where it can be obliterated in the debate by those who need persuading on the issue but will not accept the extra baggage from excess detail or high principle.

Labour came from a background of the believing the state (and from their assumptions therefore the people) should own large amounts of industry and housing. In the UK in the 1980s the Conservative government took on a privatising agenda which they believed would turn loss making industries they were having to subsidise into tax generating business, and indeed at first did. As a result they fell in love with the privatising agenda, going out of their way to look for privatisation opportunities. By the mid nineties, they privatised the railways even though in doing so they were still subsidising them, breaking their initial argument on privatisation that it was designed to force firms to run at a profit.

Labour in the 1980s reacted to this privatisation agenda by wanting to nationalise all of it back at a ridiculous cost to the public purse in buying up the shares the Conservatives had sold. They lost one election, another and another, and when they finally won they had stripped back to an agenda of nationalising nothing. However when in power, following some disasters on the railways, they renationalised the rail track which was still on a subsidy but no other industry. Their privatising opponents finally agreed and a new tradition was arrived at.

There is a lesson that things move step by step in this, but also a lesson about the herd losing their heads, and their opponents in their herd mentality going too far. Many socialists may feel that Labour sold out on privatisation, and though to their staunchest supporters they had, to the middle ground in Britain, they had not. They had raised the initial nationalisation bar too high because they were so pleased with their own (highly and so dangerously principled) arguments, lost and needed a position that was attractive to more than just their party faithful. In the meantime, because Labour had offered no effective opposition, the Conservative government had been allowed to go too far. The Labour party had been too easy to please on nationalisation, and as time went by, the sweetening revenues of privatisation allowed the Conservatives to become too easily pleased with their course of action which all resulted in a series of rail disasters.

The point of this is not that a given concept is good or bad, but by clinging too strongly to it and so letting through arguments on one word (like 'nationalisation' or 'privatisation') a good concept all too easily becomes bad.

The Party that is hardest to please is the most jealous of the old ways.

Although in Britain, the political debate displays the Conservatives as the traditional party and Labour as the opposite, nothing could be further from the truth. Labour has many of its own traditions that have developed over the course of more than a century.

Traditions are very useful at keeping a disparate bunch of unpaid volunteers together. This is simply because we can agree that something is red, but have no way of knowing what the other person is seeing, and key words on traditions keep parties together, even if what the individualls are seeing is slightly different. This certainty gets moved at the cost of a period of uncertainty as the change develops which no one likes and makes change harder.

This is amply demonstrated by the UK Conservatives inability to engage with Europe from 1990 for 15 years. The main political players in the European Union (EU) believe in a federal Europe, which the UK Conservative Party is fundamentally opposed to. This led to the Conservatives turning into almost a one issue party (No Europe, No bogus immigrants to be more precise) for a decade. The Conservatives were not communicating in Europe until the expansion of the EU opened up opportunities with similarly minded right wing parties newly liberated from the Soviet Union who did not want to lose their independence either. The Conservatives have found independent minded friends outside 'Old Europe' who it still distrusts on federalism, but has found new confidence through 'New Europe' thus maintaining its tradition of mistrusting the European 'project' whilst engaging with Europe in another way. Thus the tradition of independence was resolved by being built on by broadening the party's ties.

In persuading any party, respecting these traditions is vital to implementing change, as the people listening to the argument will know that it treads painfully close to those traditions, and are cautious in dealing with that part of the debate. This is the opposite to the party of the easily pleased who want lavish on their dreams, rather they would want to do it carefully, maybe do dry runs or pilot projects where applicable, which is often sensible, and use results to move the arguments towards their traditions. Their considerations (if they will listen to you) will be far more measured, but an anarchist prince will need to be highly measured too.

Why it is important not to please the easily pleased, rather the wary.

The party most wary of a policy that it accepts as necessary is likely to pursue the matter with the utmost caution. The other party which would probably ruin a policy because it would get over excited and go to excess. Giving a policy to the 'wrong' party is seen as treachery by those that would get carried away with a policy as they feel they 'own' it.

Politicians privately will tell you that all parties work on all things because that is what the electorate expect of them, but politicians are fickle and will cry wolf that they are the only ones that care about X Y Z. All parties need to pay attention to all the issues, but hold some as though precious unto themselves, at least publicly so that their followers don't question them. The true reason for the charge of treachery for handing over an idea to another party is politicians' lust for the things they believe are beholden unto them. This will be presented as your treachery for not giving it to 'them.' This is risible but easily believed. Of course the truth this implies is that politicians are only implementing laws for themselves and not the people they claim to represent. If it were otherwise they would be happy that a policy they believed in were implemented at all.

Opposition is necessary for any argument to be developed. This can easily be achieved within a party, however once a party that is too easily pleased takes a policy to the legislature, party votes get the principle of the argument through unchecked, even if it is disastrous. The formal opposition can only really hope to change minor details and appear good in front of the media. Therefore the party that can provide the most constructive opposition internally will likely perform better with an argument than the party that is most easily pleased.

The implications of this is that the wiser party to give an argument to, the less easily pleased, will lead to the jealousy and wrath of the party that wish the policy theirs and an anarchist prince will need to understand that unpopularity comes not only with mistakes on the job, but can also without having acted in bad faith in any way. In the moment, all are only as good as others say, and that is even more noticeable with unpopularity, especially unpopularity with the greedy and jealous.

How to make the politically impossible possible

For something to be considered politically impossible in the contextual sense of the word, there must be a group of people actually wanting it. If no one wants a change in a direction, it is just pointless. The interesting thing about a group of people wanting a policy is that on that point, with all of its assumptions, they think alike. More often than not this means that politically they group together into the same party but are not taking the argument to any other party. The anarchist prince will note that UK Conservatives who wish to reintroduce grammar (selective) schools see it as politically impossible because of the venom with which Labour oppose such a move and that they talk amongst themselves and not to Labour. The anarchist prince will also note that the Conservatives will never dare to reintroduce grammar schools, not because Labour can block every policy with votes in parliament but because of the violence of the emotions surrounding the issue. To make this impossibility a reality, any anarchist prince wishing to pursue this policy will need to work with Labour to at least placate their emotions on the subject. If this is achieved the violence against such a move would be so reduced as to make it possible.

Solving the impossible is about sufficiently winning over those who make it impossible, not the convinced that are happily talking to themselves about such a move should the environment ever allow, which it won't without communication.

An example of a way in which Labour could build on these traditions would be using test selection within a class and not between classes (for a simple generality), so that the ones finding something the easiest could help others within groups, spreading knowledge and reducing the politics of intellectual jealousy. Indeed, children like to teach each other, as shown with Computers in Indian slums[1]. However, if ever Labour did anything approaching any form of selection, the first and most important point that they would have to hammer home to their party faithful is that none of the negatives of selective discrimination would happen and a top theme would be 'No return to Grammar' or 'No one being branded a failure at 11.' Even though something would have changed, it would not have changed any tradition, because that was being built on. Meanwhile, the Conservative Party are not be trusted with selection because they are too easily pleased by that argument, and talking to them about the merits of Grammar schools might lead to a socially agreeable conversation, but no traction on the subject in the country at large.

Chapter 4: The importance of balancing forces, not trying to view them as one.

This chapter aims to make clear that politics has a basis in the methods of maths, biology and older belief systems.

Why Mathematicians are right and Fusion is wrong

If two philosophical approaches disagree, it can be tempting to take the parts of the philosophies in their stated form and try to effectively force them together. The result is that parts of at least one philosophy have been ignored or worse still twisted to fit them in with the other. This is generally because the boundaries of the philosophies in more extreme cases have not been properly defined. For example Einstein did not try to force his relativity on Newton's gravity model, he refined gravity as a model. His new model now is in competition with Quantum Mechanics and mathematicians are trying to find something underlying both, not trying to force the two into one.

Mathematicians when provided with a paradoxical situation often resolve the paradox by looking at the generality of the two competing thoughts and try to construct one that explains both. Mathematicians have a luxury, which politicians do not. If they are trying to change the generality, then they need to change the frame of reference which to other mathematicians is very clever, but to politicians is the nightmare of having to change the language of the traditions of their parties with their grass roots.

The virtuous way in any judgement is to consider everything possible and cutting out what you believe you need to. Politics lumbers you with considerations that you cannot dismiss for reasons of symbolism with your own side (and sometimes because of abject fear from the other side), and means you cannot achieve true generality because of one or more sides.

Many politicians when trying to build cross party unity look for solutions based on a fusion of words that muddies issues rather than clarifying them. In theory the politician would do well to listen to the scientist and look at what belies all sides of the argument, except he would be called a traitor for reasons of symbolism by many and worse still his own. In politics, the generality of the argument rarely overcomes the symbolic traditions of it, people know where they stand with tradition without thinking about it, a new generality takes longer to grasp. In fact Labour showed in the run up to the 1997 election that they could change their attitude from crime being a social disease to an attitude of 'tough on crime, tough on the roots of crime.' They kept some of their traditions but built on them to a new generality. It had taken them 18 years out of power to achieve this.

Why Biology teaches us to use antagonism

As physical beings, we can move around because our legs and arms move, but on a slightly deeper level, muscles pulling on joints contract and relax in order, pulling against one another antagonistically to achieve the goal of movement. The fact that the muscles are pulling against one another is of benefit to both, but the relationship is antagonistic.

One of the failures of Marx was that he saw a permanent struggle between the ruling (class) and the many. At the time he was right, there was very little social mobility, but mobility and education have increased to such an extent that many workers become managers, set up their own businesses, even go into politics. The workers may themselves become part of the ruling class and where in the past they were one of two groupings set against one another. Now there are now friendships across the groups. Antagonism is no longer about large scale revolutions, rather smaller scale. Society benefits when antagonisms work together but not destructively.

A manager can have a staff meeting and antagonism reflects itself in the airing of views and new resolves (or of course in a disastrous meeting, half the work force can resign). This is antagonism achieving new objectives. Unions are all but in name expected to sniff out Health and Safety issues in a company, the manager has operational motivations and incentives usually. However Unions can use health and safety considerations as technicalities for broader strikes. The Union being in effect trusted to health and safety is antagonistic with profit, but if properly worked out, can be of massive help too, not least in the impact of payouts due to injury.

 Back to biology, sex is an antagonistic set of motions but so is rape, and the battle of the sexes itself can be either constructive or destructive antagonistic interactions.

The importance of self sustaining systems

In biology a cell stays alive by consuming enough energy to meet its needs. Any biological system needs this (and of course the necessary chemicals) to keep itself alive. In business a company stays alive by resourcing more money than it spends so that it can pay for the upkeep of its infrastructure. A country needs the ability to get food and materials from its own land and people to survive.

 A government funded project has to make its case for the relevant money based on utility (of three areas: environmental, social, personal) that it provides. Environmental considerations are the considerations of future generations being taken in proxy by the current generation. Social considerations are the considerations of quality of life of people currently alive. Individual considerations are for the self alone.

 So building a fountain in your town meets one of these considerations (social), costs each of the individuals in taxes and is probably pretty neutral on the environment.

The more positive a policy can do in each of the three areas, the more it ultimately pays for itself and like a company but without directors, it self sustains. This is because the energies of people wanting to keep said policy are far greater than the energies of people that view it as a burden. In terms of sustainability a policy which can be shown to have utility in all three areas (environmental, social, personal) is more likely to be put into place and get built on than one that damages one or more of these areas significantly. Taxes are a burden to sustainability, social unease too whether over crime or something else, but since before the start of the 21st century we have had to look at environmental costs in relation to sustainability too. Good policy will improve some of these areas, better policy improves all three. All three cannot be improved in all situations, but the anarchist prince will note that politicians can be lazy, sometimes don't try and call something a difficult decision when it is nothing of the sort, rather an act of short term political expedience.

Why the old ways of our land are important (melding).

Melding is an ancient (and therefore anthropologically important) British Wiccan (Witch) term and is the application of scientific (rather than political) method in dealing with a social dynamic. Finding routes forward that protect all of us, it is more important what pathways do than what they 'are.' What ideas are claimed to 'be' is of no consequence if people are being destroyed as a result.

Melding is taking the energies and momentums of different strands of thought and getting them to interact, not fuse. Thoughts can be made to interact to make them self sustaining, they can be antagonistic, they can be synergetic. Job hunting training courses can be antagonistic for those finding motivation difficult, synergetic for those wanting the course to work and self sustaining if it gets people into jobs and saves on welfare. Paying people to take these courses may motivate them more, but a backlash would come from people not looking at the results of the courses, rather what the policy 'is.' There are many people who are less concerned about the tax they save in getting people into work than the tax they have to pay to facilitate this, especially if it is perceived that some of these taxes go towards 'beer.'

This balance of energies lives in a place where words matter less than the deeds that they lead to. This requires an attitude to words and fashionable consensuses that in the short term can often be seen as blasé even disrespectful to symbolic, if improperly defined, truths, and much danger can lie therein. The idea of any government policy being seen as a 'soft touch' can more undermine a policy direction than the good it does.

Well Administered Self Sustaining Systems.

Cells are all organised chemical reactions which need breathe with their local environment and need some form of energy and nutrients. It is easy to analogise this with company needing to neither destroy nor be destroyed by its local environment, materials as nutrients and the cash from sales as its energy. If either a cell runs out of energy or a company loses its cash they die.

A policy can be seen in the same way, but now the environment is a plot and people of land that it must not destroy nor be destroyed by, nutrients are policy dependant (the 'greater good,' society, development and care, cost) but energy needs defining. Energy is a unique blend of moneys gained and votes for a policy, over time periods that vary.

The job in selling any policy is to persuade the politician is to persuade them it is worth money or votes or preferably both. The issues of greater (and so pragmatic) good arise from these policies even if they do get superseded. The politician sets the precedent and even if the policy runs out of energy, if it's foundations hold up, its values become universal. That is the difference between a victory through life force and spirit living on. If a dead company lives on, it is her offshoots. A dead cell lives on it is by their offspring. If a policy lives on it is through the principles that are pragmatic which it espouses. No pragmatic policy without principle has ever survived over the course of time, nor has any policy based on principle with no idea of the practicalities. It is the structure of the anarchist prince to ensure that policies achieve both principle and pragmatism for there lies the spirit.

Chapter 5: Identity, Images and Tradition.

This chapter aims to show that identity and tradition are about imagery overlaps rather than any one overpowering truth.

More than one image holds the identity of a single metaphor

Consider Britishness and one image. It may be the Union Jack, it may be a satellite image of our island, it may be the NHS, pubs, warm summer evenings (clearly not very unique), an apple tree, flowing fields and meadows, or one of a myriad of things. It is clear that our collective image of Britishness is a mosaic of these things and we mainly subscribe to enough to find overlap with other from our own country thus giving us a feeling of oneness in the Britishness Metaphor. The images of Britishness are new and old, but most are laid down as traditional, after the political discourse has finished with that area if only for a short while.

Someone who loves cars does not hold only the image of their car, but images of driving, other cars, races, all coming down to one point, cars, again providing overlap for people to engage.

Both examples are aspects of people taking an interest in something and through a plethora of images taking ownership of a subject and relating to others through many of these images. In the world of cars, the more images you know about, the more you are deemed to 'know your cars' and so have ownership of cars that are not even yours.

Identity and Tradition and Party

Identity reaches many parts of ourselves, in relation to various topics of interest. Definitions are weak, Socialist can be anyone from Stalin and his authoritarian monstrosities, to Gorbachev and his liberal leanings[1], from Romania's Chauchescu and his corruption or genocide[2] to Czechoslovakia's Dubček and his principled stand against Russian Militarism in 1968[3]. Conservatives vary across subject, they can be political, theological and intellectual. Though Conservatism is associated with keeping the old, a radical Conservative agenda can throw out the old as did Thatcher. It is known that identity can be used to mask real intent, how many paedophiles work in children's' care to help 'protect them?' All too often because of the image and identity of their 'carers' abused children do not get believed. Similarly politicians can hide their real agenda until it is too late to stop them, Stalin being a classic point in example after being warned about in Lenin's Will over his disproportionate power base[4], he managed to make himself look very weak to his colleagues, kept position and then continued to develop his overwhelming powerbase.

Identity also hits the fourth person (I (1st), you (2nd), (s)he (3rd), abstract construct like company (4th)). Because companies are not allowed to talk each other down in advertisements, they can change their images around in a short space of time. If a company is ordered to stop anti competitive practices by the government, it is still allowed to advertise the changes as though they were their own, without any other company being able to contest those claims in any way.

Although anyone can attack a political party without being sued or incurring a legal breach (and all parties practise in misrepresenting one another), a political party can still change very quickly on the points of traditions. In 1945 the UK Conservatives lost the election to a Labour Party that wanted a welfare and healthcare state. In 1951 the Conservative Party won under Churchill supporting health care, welfare, and an accelerated house building agenda, it was also the party of the establishment. However, this would slide, first to good governance, then the party of the economy and in the 1980s it reduced itself to being the party of low taxation no longer trusted with the country's health care (despite increasing spending on it).

From the time of Thatcher through to Howard in 2005, traditional Conservatism was seen as being on the 'One Nation' wing of the party but the times of One Nation were periods harked back to with no traction beyond the occasional lip service of leaders and accepted Conservatism was the policy of perpetual cutting of taxes.

From 2005-10 things turned around in five years, One Nation in 2010 is back in The Conservative Party as 'Modern Conservatism' whilst bizarrely the 'Traditional' Conservatives of 2010 just want tax cuts. In this way between 2005 and 2010 the Conservative Party turned its traditional wing into its modern wing and vice versa. The positions of the two groups have reversed, but not their identity as Conservatives for they still have many interests that overlap.

This is why parties can update so quickly, because there are different traditions within them. Even if they share the same tradition in an overall party, like the rest of us politicians have more interests than one, more images that they identify with than one, and more loyalties than one.

Chapter 6: On why changing the system is better than in being in control of the system.

This chapter aims to establish research in politics as a valid line of approach that needs bolstering not ignoring.

Politicians, Researchers, War and Line.

Some people enter politics and get excited about the thought of a war though most do not. Someone working within the system does not need to get to a position where they have to take the drastic decisions of sanctions, especially war, at least if they are willing to swap power for influence. People in power have a limited shelf life, with their official line on a variety of subjects becoming ever harder to change the longer they continue. People with influence need people or groups of people with power to listen to them but cannot take a country to war, nor be expected to. Both politicians and researchers can make comebacks, but researchers more so, because they do not have to have a public line, and can be seen as having hit and miss ideas even when some of their perceived misses are in fact hits. A politician cannot make nearly as many mistakes whilst holding onto their position.

If an anarchist prince wants one policy carved in their image, they will need power to get every detail they desire. If an anarchist prince wishes to help overall with a myriad of policies they will need influence but not necessarily power.

The importance of not having a line

Once a line is publicly defined, it can rarely be reversed. If a researcher comes out with a load of rubbish their boss or bosses just tell them so and as long the virtuous work outweighs the dross, the boss will put with this more than once. If a researcher establishes a public line out of tune with their boss, the researcher either retracts, walks or is sacked. If the researcher burbles this line in private, they are noted but not a threat to authority because they still have no public line. The result is twofold, politicians concentrate on their line and will compete to get good researchers, and researchers can playfully speak about ideas to the point of near insolence and instead of being sacked they get feedback which helps their imagination to grapple with concepts.

Why researchers outlast leaders

Researchers can work for many leaders. Leaders work for one group of people, the electorate. Once a leader's time has come there is very rarely a comeback, the political career of a politician is a conveyor belt and after they fall off the end, there is very rarely a comeback. Yeltsin managed to make a comeback in Russia after resigning from Gorbachev's team and some blame him for the dismantling of the Soviet Union. Salmond resigned as leader of the Scottish Nationalist Party, but the dearth of oratorical talent without him meant that he was invited back by his party with their hope of dismantling the United Kingdom.

Researchers are not commodities with lines, like politicians. They can work for more than one politician, if they come up with a good idea they can give it to a current politician on another part of the career conveyor belt, thus extending their life spans as researchers. They do not get the glory or wages of a leader, but if virtuous they can keep their career going longer as they are effective and do not need to set out personal lines that they may later regret. The environment does from time to time change and lucky the person who can change their line with it, maybe not so with the researcher, but certainly so with the politician.

The importance of parties ring fencing research and originality

If a political party is given money, most goes on administration and political advertising. Very little goes to research, and for every extra million raised over budget, almost all of it is earmarked for advertising. Quality of product (research) is not held in high esteem compared to the advertising of any product. Ring fencing a percentage of funds over a threshold (to not hinder smaller parties) is a simple way of ensuring that money gets spent on research.

Of course reactive policy development, or that of the politician's (and not researcher's) whims is lesser use to the anarchist prince than going in their own direction. Too much political research can be reactively aimed at justifying present political positions. Often comparatively little time is spent pro actively developing policy in as an imaginative way as possible. Paid researchers are told what to research by the boss who pays them, but they are often the best researchers yet their imaginations are wasted.

An way around this can be easily organised by allowing individuals and teams of researchers one day a week off to go where no politician's line would dare to go. Sometimes, but not always, they would be likely to bring back some useful ideas for said politician(s). The cost of this would be that for five days paid, instead of the politician getting five days traditional work, they would only get four, but the opportunity for originality, so often lost in politics, would be massively increased.

Chapter 7: Loyalty

This chapter aims to get the reader to realise that if they are to go off on an intellectual limb, then they need emotional bonds with those they are trying to persuade and loyalty is essential to overcome the dangers of division over this.

Why it is important for an Anarchist Prince to be loyal

Loyalty has the purpose of engendering trust. Loyalty extends between people and through metaphors of groups. These metaphors can be the golf club, political, friends from college and so on. When power is involved the allegiance to a metaphor means that though all are loyal to that metaphor, they still may form into groups within it. This can easily become destructive without strong leadership as can be seen by infighting in political parties as often happens whilst leadership is weak. Being seen as loyal to the cause is vital in times when leadership is not strong nor success great. Loyalty can be both to people and the cause. If you are seen as loyal to others, they will tend to be loyal to you, if you are not seen to be loyal they will more easily turn on you. Any anarchist prince will be an individualist in relation to the grouping that they have joined (if not and they agree with all the group, then they are not an anarchist prince in relation to that group and could do well persuading other groups). However, this individuality is dangerous in any group psychology. People are generally not stupid and if you are loyal it will catch up with your shadow in time just as if you are disloyal. Therefore due to individuality the need for the anarchist prince to be loyal to the group is all the greater, as well as the need to remind them that all have (at least some) mutual values.

Why individuality needs loyalty

Silence unites and words divide. Similarly, individuality in any group can allow the individual much movement. However, as with different words, different characteristics divide. Individuality can be accepted if there is sufficient likeability as well as trust (gained through loyalty) both of which more often than not are two way streets. A group will have a tendency to coalesce behind views both right and wrong. To agree where a group is right is easy, to disagree where a group is wrong is fraught with danger. It is important in these situations to show loyalty to the group by acknowledging where or on what principles they are right but then to go on and extend the arguments. Beyond this, the rules on numbers are simply they are many, you are one. This individual position means you need people within the group to feel rapport with you, through loyalty and like, before they will spend their time listening to your minority view. With no loyalty or mutual like, there is much less chance of the group accepting, trusting or respecting your individual position.

On how trust is not formed through allegiance rather giving to the others.

On joining an allegiance, the first question at the back of the minds is 'do we trust them.' This is not particularly bad, it is generally expressed through people being friendly and a normal get to know you session. If people consider you to be suitable for the allegiance, then they will deal with you as anyone else and you gradually form your friendships with people you have rapport with.

Trust between individuals increases the more that they see each other working for the team. It is expressed as working for the cause, but the emotions are really gained from giving to the overall team effort. This can easily be gained through regular support and campaigning. The more individual you are, the more you will need to be seen campaigning on doorsteps through wind, rain, sleet and snow. An anarchist prince would do well to remember that others accepting your individuality is them giving to you and you need to give back, through the team to maintain acceptance and favour within the team.

Capitalising Trust and Favour

In politics, you need to either advance the position of yourself or the ideas you espouse.

 The traditional political path is to advance yourself into position to be able to enact what you will. If your ideas are not abrasive in any way, this means getting to a position of responsibility in any administration. If your ideas are abrasive then you need to get yourself in control of that aspect of the administration to have any hope of getting the policies through. The implementation of the less abrasive ideas requires lower position so the difficulty in getting there is not as great as getting to the higher position required for the more abrasive ideas.

An alternative approach (The Anarchist's Approach) is to ignore your position in relation to the arguments and look at the position of the arguments you wish implemented. If you can persuade someone who is in position the merits of a case, how it is in their interests to deal with it (power, glory, naked self interest) and that they can persuade others of these considerations, the ideas may be of interest to them. Allowing them control over any favour that may arise deems your own position irrelevant to the agenda that you are dealing with. However in communicating any such ideas, it is necessary to build a reputation within the team of a constructive and team working attitude. Individualism needs to be balanced within a team and the anarchist prince should understand this: The anarchist prince should be seen to be working through the team at all times.

As a final note, do not expect your first attempts at policy argumentation to get heard (though they may) it can take experience, perseverance and reputation building within the group and feedback, often over years.

"There is no limit to what a man can do or how far he can go if he doesn't mind who gets the credit." Robert W. Woodruff.

Chapter 8: Power and Conveyor Belts

This chapter aims to show that people in high power are prone to not see it as service, rather a nice little earner and that they need limited shelf lives to reduce this tendency.

The implications of power and of not having it

If it is better in the moment to be feared than to be loved, then power is essential. However power corrupts and service to society requires humility. Of course any person who thinks that they know what is better for society than the state of development so far, has arrogance (for believing they know better especially when they are starting out) and power magnifies this. The danger of magnifying this arrogance leads to the loss of human touch that the shaper of the law has, but lack of power leaves that individual in need of influence with the powerful. Helping one powerful group of people means you risk being attacked by another powerful group with competing interests as 'the friend of my enemy is my enemy.' Power exists and people will fight for it without care for anyone other than themselves and their close ones, even in a democracy the cliques that run a country are often in reality of few in number. People will use power to destroy for reasons good, bad, ugly and petty. When engaging with politics having power protects you but not having it is a potential peril to yourself.

However not having power also means that an anarchist prince is in a position to do the work that interests her, whatever the risks. Having power means having to make decisions about random issues from people you are responsible for as the issues turn up. This can take up much time and like the work of the anarchist prince can also blow up in your face, not for giving ideas to the 'wrong people' but genuinely making a mistake in a decision you have to undertake on a subject you know little or nothing about.

The importance of power allowing progress

If a grouping in power do not allow progress and are seen to consistently block it, then slowly wrath will build up and often the result is either that power base being broken or the use of tyranny to keep it. The UK House of Lords in the early 20th Century was dominated by Conservative Peers and was blocking all legislation that it did not like from the elected government. This led to an impasse between Liberals and Conservatives over a budget that led to two general elections on the whole matter, which the Conservatives did not win[1].

The Liberals were in a position to ask King George V to appoint a mass of Liberal peers, which the King made clear he was willing to do. The result was that the Conservatives split, and House of Lords accepted that it had advisory powers on financial matters but could not indefinitely block legislation through the acceptance of the Parliament Act[2]. This takes Machiavelli who pointed out that no one person should have ultimate blocking power, and extends it into no one grouping having this power without recourse to the people in elections.

Why power should only be used temporarily

Politicians traditionally like to refer to their work as service, but privately they refer to it in terms of their careers. Jury service is for two weeks and there are no lucrative side projects that can be taken on because of this. By 2009 it became very clear that the overwhelming number of our Members of Parliament were wrongly (and a good number fraudulently) claiming expenses to make as much out of their jobs as possible for themselves, not concentrating on what they could with their jobs for others[3]. There are precedents in political parties whereby someone can hold a local position (or role) for only a fixed amount of time, but the moment that the role involved becomes a paid role, this precedent vanishes quite quickly. This equates to the less power and money involved in a position, the more it is seen as service, but the more power and money involved it becomes a career where service can all too easily be forgotten. This does not mean that all in higher position become corrupt, but the tendency has been well known for some time.

A way to deal with this is to make position held at all levels in a party being of a finite duration and if that time passes, the politician either progresses or resigns from that level. If they desire to continue in politics, they can find another level where their tenure has not been used up.

Consider a member of parliament being only allowed to sit for thirteen years. That Member of the UK Parliament could use up three of thirteen years and that would leave ten years of that quota. They could then work for five years as a minister in the government using up some of that quota, and drop back to be a Member of Parliament with the remaining ten years of that member of parliament quota still intact. This shortens shelf lives of those who do not move on and would force people to see their work as a period of service and so stop some of the dangers of corruption. This does lead to increased turnover but turnover of politicians and ideas are for the benefit of society as a whole, it should be remembered that when a member of parliament sees no personal progress, they can easily get bored, politicians do plot and the devil makes work for empty hands.

Ideas come from each generation as they grapple to understand the world in which they live, as created by their elders and forebears. The purpose of politics should be the progression of these ideas, rather than the elders using fraternity to hold down these ideas. The ideas of the next generation are in no small part to deal with the problems that their elders created, every solution creates its own problems, unless it is an extremely good solution. Elders will know that their fraternities are rapport based as they have political lines to hold. Currently they cannot easily get voted out of a particular position in a party because they have the position and offer continuity with the past which always makes taking people with outlandish outlooks on board a difficulty. However elders will also know that we rarely see the shit on our own shoes and each generation thinks it was the best.

The anarchist prince will note that by knocking elders off the conveyor belt, new ideas and people will get put in place more readily. Elders will know that if this process happens too quickly that a party becomes rudderless and with no clear direction, dangerous.

As final notes on members of parliament serving no more than certain length terms, first a party leader will likely also want a finite number of people that they may make exempt at any given time for reasons both of excellence and loyal voting fodder. Second, it may be wise for a member of parliament who has finished their time to wait for normal elections before resigning, rather than just forcing frequent local elections which would undermine the main elections of the people making a decision about their government.

Chapter 9: Information

This chapter aims to show the power of information to the point where the controllers of information need to be balanced and controlled as a strand of the constitution.

The press and literacy

Following the import of the printing press to Western Europe, newspapers started sporadically. However the power of this method of communication was not to be fully harnessed until it was enjoyed by the many and not just the few. There were two components to this, cost of the newspaper and levels of literacy in the population. The cost came down first by the mid nineteenth century and the growth of education saw literacy levels go up. This was to give means of distributing information and opinion in a one directional way (from the few writing the newspaper to the many reading it) for a populace to develop both knowledge but also start grouping by opinion, especially in societies as they developed to one man one vote. Where the press has informed and entertained it has also motivated literacy and helped the government to keep people up to date with developments, even if the government sometimes may not wish for the free press any or all of the time.

Electronic communication

Electronic communication surpasses the printed press in four ways, first the speed with which it can disseminate information. Second (though newspapers do have letters pages) massively increase the two way dynamic of the passage of information, which in effect turns communication from one to many, to many to one (with newspapers) to many to many with connected computer communication. Third, electronic information gives us not only the ability to store huge amounts of information (libraries have achieved this since the times of the ancients) but also the ability to access that information both highly specifically and extremely quickly. Fourth, electronic communication is massively cheaper than previous forms of communication. This in turn allows the many not only to research or verify facts, but communicate them with each other at immense speeds. This is of more concern to some governments, who wish their interpretations of events and not their opponents to be heard[1] than to others, who let most information pass freely. However, all governments monitor this activity which is one step from blocking it. The more we become reliant on electronic information we become, the more powerful our understanding can be, but the more easily our governments can monitor us: the saying 'if you have nothing to hide you have nothing to fear' is often employed by politicians to the people, but when it comes to finding out the affairs of government, it turns out that politicians have much to fear and hence so do the people have much to fear from politicians as a group whether or not an individual politician has anything to hide.

Dangers of groups and subgroups

When there is one newspaper, there is little competition in opinion, where there are many examples and forms of communication people identify themselves within groupings, largely following a specific grouping of influences. People use the newspapers that they read as part of their identity, and although the newspapers do not openly attack one another, they do hold the lines of the political positions that they represent. The upshot is that on one issue, two separate people reading two separate newspapers not only form different opinions, but the facts that they rely on can have little overlap if it all. This in the long run does not help political discourse, or the passage of ideas between groupings, rather through identity helps divide our society with no hope for feedback.

Seeing is believing on a massive scale

Libel laws were set up because people behind newspapers had the power to disseminate lies at a rate that word of mouth would only ever be able to achieve during a demonstration or riot. An example of the power of the media was demonstrated in 1990 where The Sun newspaper (through an article headlined 'Up Yours Delors[2,3]' aimed at getting people to give a two fingered salute at France because Jacques Delors was French, even though he was working as the head of the European Commission in Belgium. Indeed The Sun prides itself on being able to win elections through its communications[4].

 Arguably it tries to be responsible about this, but the decision as to what 10 million people read on a daily basis out of a total electorate of 45 million, (equating to more than 20%) is decided by one man, it's owner. It is comparatively of little consequence that he acts with good faith, it is of consequence that there is nothing to stop him doing otherwise.

Why the Media as a constitutional Strand must itself be checked.

The media has come to a point where governments employ people to manage their media relations. This demonstrates the fear that governments feel about the media. The government is a strong constitutional strand but on a daily basis fears the media. Further in a free society the government cannot control the media. The media therefore have the power to daily affect a constitutional strand, but should not be interfered with in their own right which makes them de facto a constitutional strand in their own right. Every constitutional strand needs to be checked and the media are no exception. As government cannot rightly control the media, the media needs them divided within, yet able to come together as a responsible if divided collective. We will come to this.

Dividing, conquering and empowering large scale media

Media structures in the UK are top down, one to many, whereas the rest of communication structures are becoming more many to many. Journalists enter the profession as idealists only to have to tow the line of the newspaper owner without any right to input themselves. Owners need to make a profit, need control over advertising and the structure of the paper (allotment to news, views, sport and so on). However the content can easily be managed by an editor (and possibly also sub editors) who can be elected by the owner and media staff in an electoral college. In other words this involves making the media democratic. This would be a mechanism whereby an elected editor could show independence of an owner but would need a large majority of the (voting) journalists behind that decision if the owner had a large block vote.

 The purpose of this would be to give more staff an input into the position of a newspaper than a disproportionate amount of influence being given to one person (the owner) with the inherent imbalances in point of view. It would also allow journalists to more easily try to unpick an issue from various different points of view as a service to their readers, as opposed to holding one leadership (owner's) line which often educates no one. In effect this would be to turn newspapers into hierarchical democracies with the staff taking on more responsibility for their views on the direction of their media outlet (newspaper, TV channel) or leave it to a strong editor as they see fit.

 This argument is not to say that political groupings of newspapers are wrong at all, rather by opening the direction of development to more people a in a newspaper, it may become far more inclusive of views not entirely traditional to them at all. It should be noted that in such a system, potential new employees for a paper may need to be politically vetted as well tested in other ways to help maintain the newspaper's identity.

American Football's lessons for the media being the watchman of both government and itself

The structure of the American Football National Football league is unusual for a money making corporation. It is in effect a cooperative of clubs. The idea is simple, the League is a company, which owns a majority share in each of the clubs 70% and the owner owns 30% of the club. Each club owns an equal share in the league and between them all of the shares. For a new owner to be able to take a club, the league, or committee of club owners have to vote in favour of it[5]. The result is that the league as a whole can exercise control as to who may be a club owner. If one chairman embarrasses the league to a sufficient extent, the other chairmen can vote him out of control of that club and if the individual is unwilling to sell his shareholding, they can appoint others to run the club during the impasse.

The media can similarly be legislated to have to form a holding company which needs no more than running costs to have a majority shareholding in each newspaper that it holds. It is imperative that government control over the media is restricted, but the media need the tools to be able to regulate themselves, namely overwhelming majorities of media owners being able to come together and remove people from owning newspapers. In reality the threat would work most of the time. However if the media are to be expected to exercise responsibility there is need for some sanction if they do not because otherwise sales will override all. This is a concept about making media owners accountable and can be seen in the spirit of Magna Carta, where people (or papers) are accountable to their peers. For reasons of stability and of liberty, people should be accountable to their peers through the newspaper holding groups, not government as that is a separate constitutional strand. Clearly newspapers fall into natural political groupings. To avoid potential political fighting, the media may need more than one group of newspapers tied together. If other newspapers in a grouping came together against the behaviour of one it would much less likely be tarnished with the accusations of political games. This mechanism of joint ownership can also be used to help hapless owners with the removal of editors that they in no way want but the staff overwhelmingly voted in, giving ultimate power back to the owners through collective responsibility.

It should be noticed that controllers of data used by the government could also be made accountable to their peers in this way, as other forms of media.

On how a government demanding our transparency needs to be transparent in its approach

Information is not just media however, information massively affects what a government can know about us. No one wants to be watched or have their private matters being monitored by the state, however the government now with mobile technology can even track us. The state on the other hand wants no one being a danger to either itself or others. The ability for the state to take liberties is necessary to stop harming of other lives, property and now the environment. However if these powers are granted to the state without constraints, people acting in the name of the state, like all others will overstep the mark. It is easy for the state to freely ask questions, but it is imperative that we know what it is asking, when and why. If knowledge is power, then the state by asking questions is amassing this power which needs to be known, checked and checked if abused. For any government to retain the high ground in their use of information, people need to be able to watch what they are doing (even if in generality), whether legitimately or where it happened illegitimately (in specific cases).

The moral of this is that if an individual needs to be responsible to maintain his or her rights, then for any high ground, so does the state and more accurately the people acting in the name of the state. This has been the case for many years, but is far more exaggerated now with the amount of data and speed of analysis that governments now have. Ultimately this transparency in the use of data will make our government either empower or destroy us. Without transparency, the power of the knowledge involved will corrupt people to overstep the mark, become corrupt and we will have no way of knowing.

This should be sufficient argument that suppliers of data (from newspapers to government databases), like the judiciary, need to be constitutionally separate from the government to maintain a transparent link and be able to rebuke the government without fear or favour.

Chapter 10: Mathematics and predictions thereof

This chapter aims to show the power of maths, and the dangers of not seeing it as an assumption based tool, rather all powerful.

Understanding Math

Maths has underpinned all of the sciences, from studying the stars and engineering achievements in older civilisations, some methods which we struggle to understand now, through to modern physics, electronics, chemistry, biology and even social understandings. It has concepts such as imaginary numbers which simply do not exist, but can help with calculations nevertheless. It helps us understand gradients, volumes, forces and pressures. Math is instrumental in all computers and the applications that they support, as well as understanding whether data supports an underlying hunch about the subject which it describes through statistics.

Politicians are known to site 'lies, damned lies and statistics' but what they site are not statistics. A statistic is not a total (unless the whole population is counted) but an estimate of a total from a sample, critically with error margins. Politicians are not known to have any mathematical virtuosity, and less still with admitting to error, which is why they will fail to quote error margins, they don't understand the maths sufficiently to realise the need for humility and admission of error. Every mean has a variance or error.

It is sad that the understanding of maths is desired by so few, it underpins most if not all of the technology that we have, but learning it at school is comparatively dry, with example after example to be solved with precious few applications and students not encouraged to help and motivate one another with group problem solving 'investigations.'

Understanding possibilities underpinned by Math

Applications in maths are of the type, 'if a man rows up a river at 3 miles per hour and the river flows down at 1.5 miles per hour, what is his overall speed?' The final calculations are the mechanics of maths but what sets them up is what is known as a 'model.' In this case, the man rows at 3mph relative to the water, but the water flows at 1.5mph relative to the bank, setting up the final calculation of the rower's speed relative to the bank being overall speed=3mph-1.5mph which is then solved. Every application of maths is underpinned by a model based on a set of assumptions about reality (prone to error or over simplification). The calculations can then be given to mathematicians who will either solve them (generally correctly) or tell you that (s)he can't. It is the models that drive forward new theories which can lead to new technologies, but it is the models that are most fraught with danger (though the maths itself may possibly be wrong though this is highly unlikely in any given group reviewed calculation). Therefore we need to concentrate on the models, which require assumptions about the reality they claim to represent and often do not.

On Assumptions and Nature

The most understanding of math is the understanding of how to generalise but not over generalise. This is not just a mathematical problem, racism, sexism indeed all forms of tribalism are examples of attempts to generalise but end up being over generalised. This occurs in the world of words. When we try to form a generality we either do so consciously or subconsciously. We have evolved over hundreds of millions of years to subconsciously generalise: Dogs are dogs, we recognise them yet their shapes and sizes are such that it is a wonder that we so successfully do, which in the main we do. Conscious generalisation is the product of conscious thought and our skills in it are so poor that we have used generalisations to justify anything even highly wrong, most recently Apartheid, most violently Hitler's problem with the Jews.

Just because we seek to explain something scientifically instead of qualitatively does not mean that our ability to generalise is any better. The process is stripped down and we have to make assumptions about reality. These assumptions need to be accurate as inaccuracies can multiply up in the resulting maths. However these assumptions also need to stand the test of time or adjust with time. In engineering and the design of new buildings and bridges, assumptions are made about subject matter as emotionally evocative as concrete, steel, bricks and building plans in understanding what amount of abuse these structures can take. Yet engineers always add in large error factors because they know that they cannot trust their assumptions to generalise fully with nature interacting with them. However self doubt in assumptions is not always the case. Whereas the engineer will put in errors about their assumptions about materials, social scientists can use assumptions about people that simply defy reality. In societal modelling the concept of negative liberty is used to build our stable society. In negative liberty humans are assumed to have no altruism at all, because the positive liberty of 'acting' in other's interests can and has led to abuse (though how neglect in society is also abuse should be considered by the anarchist prince also). Negative Liberty is also deemed useful because it makes the equations of this bizarre 'society' work even though the assumptions about humans are completely unnatural.

The problem facing both positive and negative Liberty can be summed up as: You can kill someone with cotton wool, but the complete lack of it kills them too. However it is mathematical considerations, not human considerations which has led positive liberty to be effectively thrown out of the window when modelling human nature.

The precision of infinity

Infinity is a concept that frightens most. Mathematically it is not about 'What comes after the edge of the universe?' 'And after that?' 'And after that?' and so on. It is more about following a trail of numbers and showing that no matter how high the numbers are, there are always higher numbers further down the sequence. If this is done with time, it is a way of saying that the numbers will always get higher with time. If high numbers represent success and low numbers failure in some test, the numbers permanently getting higher over time are saying that the structure will be successful over all time.

Though this may seem a strange way to pursue matters (no structure will last an infinite amount of time, the sun will burn the whole planet up one day). However to mathematicians it is surprisingly seductive because from their point of view with their assumptions about some reality and their calculations they have shown that for the foreseeable future some results will hold true. This is the result of equations based on some assumptions about reality giving us a prediction into the future that is potentially useful.

There is a further caveat, often mathematically if trying to prove something will hold 'infinitely' expressions tend to cancel out and disappear far more easily than when calculating for finite time. And any mathematician who is honest will tell you that some expressions taking each other out are far more pleasant than expressions that need to be solved for. In other words, an equation claiming to hold infinitely is often easier to solve than one which talks about a finite amount of time, but like all humans mathematical modellers can be lazy and take the easier route. This is not to say that the mathematical use of infinity is always wrong, it is not, but in the context of biology it can be a very dangerous cop out.

Negative Liberty was used as a way of developing a stable society, but the assumption that humans want to, and do, help each other for no gain, which is true on occasion in all societies, was messing up the equations. So the theorists came up with a stunning idea, work on the assumption that this is a nothing for nothing society and see if the equations predicted a stable society then. Our society was then modelled as a game of poker where no one helps each other, in fact that would be cheating (even within families) if we helped one another. The result of this selfish society was that modellers got a result that 'held' for all time (infinity) and successive Western civilisations have endorsed concepts such as 'there is no such thing as society' 'greed is good' as a means of ensuring this stability whilst the poor have gotten poorer. Indeed the very right wing politicians who have are trying to model our society as being one of no altruism are the ones who argue against the state fulfilling that role. Aside from the tragedy of this, there is a deeper lesson for politicians: If the equations work for the assumptions then good, if not, then bad, but never should the assumptions work for the equations. This is especially true when we start negating obvious basic assumptions. Politicians worry about exactitude with basic physical or chemical models, they do not want chemical factories blowing up, and will put error margins in to ensure that. However politicians will strip out truths about biological reality because they are unpredictable, chaotic and therefore impossible to fully model over time with certainty.

The seduction of a result that would last for an infinite time (whilst no society does) can be too much for policy developers because they want certainty, to be seen to be certain, want a certain society and yet do not understand that which underpins these results is not itself certain. Or as with modelling society with no altruism, flat wrong.

Please note that if a sequence is to converge to infinity, then every test number must show a case where there has to be a minimum step in the sequence whereupon that and every subsequent step in the sequence are greater than the test number (by at least a given finite amount). The example above only alluded to infinity to keep the reading (comparatively) light. It is not wasted on the author that although math has many powers, one of its greatest is to bore.

The power of infinity and the greater power of self correction

There is another way around this. In Britain we don't vote a government in for infinite time, we have the right to chop and change every five years. In this way, the policy makers can learn from the people and look for societal models that will hold up for 50 years, like repairs on an old building. Then after 35 years take another look and do what needs to be done. This doesn't have the appeal of a society that will 'last 1,000 years' but then to date many have tried, none have succeeded and their successors changed the plans anyway. Bizarrely, though societal modellers refuse to acknowledge self correction, satellites in space do exactly that, errors magnify and constant reappraisal of velocity and position are required to keep the trajectory of satellites on course. In the same way we revaluate where we are in business, games and so on, yet when modelling society this is all too easily discarded. Alas, nothing is certain forever.

Chapter 11: Confrontation of large and small, the powerful or the non powerful.

This chapter aims to show that big is not best, small is important too.

The Age Of Power And Scale

When the industrial revolution occurred, most of the work force had been on the land with no need for extra skills or education. The second agricultural revolution had freed up much labour and they went to work in the mines and the towns. Conditions were appalling and whereas before these peoples' grandparents had their own bit of land, these people had nothing. Many tin miners had to pay for their equipment including explosives from the mine the result of which was that if they did not push back the face sufficiently, they could end the week in debt to the pit owners despite their many hours and much toil[1]. Coalminers pooled their money to pay for libraries[2], likely in the hope of improving their positions so that their children may not have to spend a life down the pit. Karl Marx had different ideas and saw power in the hands of the proletariat as opposed to the bourgeoisie and developed a political philosophy around it, namely the Communist Manifesto[3].

Adolf Hitler gave a response to this putting power in the hands of the select, with the traditions of warring between the two sides remaining to this day. The purpose of this section is not to discuss the merits or otherwise of either Communism or Fascism, rather to notice their reliance on the scale of the state as both Marx and Hitler claimed that their ways granted supreme power to their states and that it was up to people to uphold these states (collectives or empires) for their own safety.

The implications of reliance on the scale and power of the state are that the state must be upheld at all costs. These philosophies instead of liberating people made them de facto slaves to the state. Of course human nature never fully complies with all norms and the result of any confrontation between these and the perceived needs of the state led to the individual being placed in much peril to the point of capital. Hitler killed 6 million Jews, Stalin 50 million of his own and Pol Pot killed over one million of his own[4] with crimes including 'being educated' with all the dangers that that brought to the state.

As an aside, it should be noted that when the state is deemed objective, then human subjectivity is quickly forgotten. The state is a subjective system made by people but alas not necessarily for people, rather one person's 'vision' of how we should all live or worse still just a few people's interests. Neither communism nor fascism allowed for the age old saying 'there's now't so queer as folk,' and any system not allowing for individuality eventually loses the trust of the many as individual needs, desires and modes of self expression arise.

The Age of Miniaturisation

The second world war gave the world two gifts, the nuclear bomb and the victory of scale but at the same time the very basic computer and the start of technology using its power to shrink rather than expand things. As the world recovered from this in the 1950's people in the West had an education, lighting and more money while printing costs were coming down. People started to read more, ideas started circulating, the contemporary culture grew while people were being asked to take responsibility and empower their lives. The result of this was that societal and slowly legal norms started to give us more and more space. It should not be underestimated that not only did we see computers, new medications, genetic modifications for all of the power of the minute, but also the photo of the Earth taken from the Moon giving us another view of our own planet as small. We have slowly become aware of the importance of small things being as important as the big and this has impacted on social policy to take into account the needs of the small (individual people). The second world war completed the victory of scale and started the victory of the minute.

Why Human Constructs should work for us

It is quite clear to people in the 21st Century that a policy has to work for both the scale (state, society, community) but also the minute (people, minorities, habitats). This indicates a need for a symbiosis between the natural (individual people, the environment) and any system they are expected to uphold. It must work if not to the interest, then not to the detriment of either side. This applies to the state and noticeably also economic policy. If people were slaves to the state under Communism or Fascism, then it should be noticed that they can also be a slave to The Economy in free market economics. Debt is the main burden when interest rates ensure that none of the original capital of a loan is paid off as is the case for many countries in the 'developing world' which are simply not developing because of all their debt. Loan sharks are the equivalent developed country scourge, again picking on people or groupings with comparatively little money or power. The 'economy' is not working for these people, even when they are acting in the best of faith, which any virtuous legal system, or other system working within it (health, economy) should.

Laws in the interests of the incumbent state versus the interests of the people

The easiest laws to enact are the most generalised. One simple rule (e.g. premeditated murder) and we have no problems beyond that. Unfortunately the affairs of the state are more complicated than that, yet the law is a very blunt instrument. Tax is one example of cat and mouse where the government of the day and accountants working for the corporations are in a constant battle to maximise revenues (for the state or the accountant's client). Controls over everyday human behaviour, because of its varied and chaotic nature, are infinitely more complex.

The nature of party politics is to try to hold the interests of various groupings within the party together, and as silence unites and words divide, it is easier to come up with a few simple (if coarse) rules than a complicated analysis whilst keeping your party together. In 1987 The UK Conservative Party were elected with a manifesto commitment to a 'Community Charge,' less affectionately known as the 'Poll Tax.' It was beautifully simple to legislate, each local authority set a flat annual local tax payment. This was to be paid by each person in that borough, with students and those out of work paying 20% of this value. The resulting application was a disaster. 1 million refused to pay for its relative inequity, it was an utterly regressive tax, there were riots the worst of which saw 300 protesters and 300 police injured while miraculously no one was killed and due to its link to the electoral register (this was used to identify potential non-payers) over a million gave up their right to vote. It cost the Prime Minister her job, and skewed the next general election in favour of the Conservatives who had put in place this nightmare, many could not financially afford to pay the tax so they could not vote against the party that had implemented it. This 'Poll Tax' was so unacceptable that it was dismantled with a legally more complicated but fairer Council Tax, because so many simply would not accept this Poll Tax. However, if the people had accepted it, Margaret Thatcher would have succeeded in removing 1 million people who voted against her from the electoral register legally, and no minister at the time worked very hard in public to allow these people a vote.

Law makers acting on behalf of the state should note that if they make something simple for themselves, it does not mean that it necessarily follows that it is easy for others to abide by. This is particularly true of prohibitions and taxes which need a consensual population to easily police. However, as we have discussed before, politicians can be lazy and it may not be in their immediate interests to tease out a law. For example after a terrorist atrocity, it is better to look strong, firm and authoritative (which wins votes), with no real need in getting to the bottom of the issue other than where to hit back. This is not cynical about politicians, rather the environment they work in, they're more protected by their own party if they drop a hammer and look firm in the face of a danger (which has already happened), because contemplation can easily be mistaken for dithering and so can lose votes.

In all cases, the interests of the politicians (claiming to act in the interests of the state and/or people) and the interests of the people are not necessarily the same. Therefore the cynicism of politicians towards the people and vice versa is sometimes justifiable but sometimes is just unacceptable bad faith.

Good Faith, Bad Faith, Corruption and Power

This chapter supposes that the state is acting in the name of the state (even if the state is some representation of the peoples' will). The individual acts in their own right. Reality dictates that individuals try to alter the state and the state the individual or societal groups to which belong to it. It is all too often true that those acting in the name of the state are lining their nests so that whilst claiming to act in the name of the state they corrupt that to the interests of their family, lovers and friends. The state in Fascist or Communist, Democratic and Free Market philosophy is that, claiming to act in the interests of a greater whole, but in reality is much more to do with the people responsible for acting in these names ending up only acting in their own interests. A state geared to the individuals is as important as galvanising individuals to be part of a greater system, but all too often politicians can look at it one way or the other, not often enough to both.

Chapter 12: On A Few Matters Relating to War

This chapter aims to introduce the reader to some basic non violent concepts that are needed to win any war.

The greater the cultural differences the greater the respect or tyranny needed to win

History has largely been confined to areas of the world until the age of the sea empire. Except for the wars between the Christians and the Muslims, most popular history in Europe was about one country invading the next. If you were invaded, chances were that you shared aspects of your religion, traded with these people before and were asked to do little more than pay tax.

The age of the sea empire ensured that peoples were coming together who had culturally separated at least thousands of years before. The Europeans who were exploiting these other continents had also developed the gun which was of such military significance that they could use firepower alone to keep most peoples down. There was not much need for respect, tyranny worked: On the Banda Islands the Dutch did not have warm relations from the outset, the Dutch got a monopoly treaty on their spices for minimal costs which led to tensions that built up to the point where the Bandanese rose up and killed 40 of the Dutch. The response from Holland took a while to prepare, but with the resulting new treaty in place, they felt vindicated in massacring over 80% of the population, leaving the remainder in such fear that they capitulated to Dutch terms[1,2]. The problem with this approach today is that the United Nations and other world powers in this age of communication, working on basic human rights would simply not accept this form of behaviour. Therefore the tyranny required to break a people in this way is (fortunately) not currently possible.

The essential problem with invading a country is that the invaders (rightly or wrongly) feels that they have the moral high ground. This is especially true of the troops, the leader may be thinking about other motives and merely feeding his men propaganda. This means that the people coming face to face with the locals feel superior at least morally and by implication feels that the invaded are inferior. The tyranny required to force capitulation is impossible but the respect required to win goodwill is undermined by a supremacist and so arrogant attitude.

Winning the war by winning the peace

This is a matter for generals but ultimately to win a battle the general needs fast moving and concentrated firepower combined with the judgement of the control structure that can unleash this firepower. To win a war you need your enemy to no longer wish to do battle with you. Not surprisingly the most important skills in winning the battle are very similar to those winning the war, clarity so that both your soldiers and the enemy understand the directives, judgement so that you do not expect too much of anyone and consistency so that people know where they stand with you.

The easiest way to achieve these three qualities is to set out your demands before the war, stick to these demands wherever possible and use judgement where changing these demands. The first two most can do, the third requires leadership which not all possess and not much can be done about.

The Allies at the end of World War I crippled Germany in the Treaty of Versailles by attempting to get them to pay for the most expensive war up to that point in history. This was not just immediately set for over 60 years of reparations for the war, far longer than any country will accept with stretches of German land being demilitarised ad infinitum and the resulting indignation led almost directly to Hitler achieving power. Far too much was expected of the Germans. No respect had been shown, no understanding of the fact that retribution must be swift for people to accept in the long term. Meanwhile Hitler achieved two things of note, World War II and the holocaust of the Jews.

 When the Allies won the war this time, Germany was split into American, British, French and Russian zones. The allies worked together to document the Holocaust and whilst high level figures were convicted of their crimes, ordinary soldiers were just made to watch a film about what had been done to the Jewish People in their names. Many left stone silent, ,many in tears. The Allies knew that they did not have to do much more than appeal to the consciences of these people for them to accept defeat and moral defeat too. They showed them respect.

 Within the zones Germany was split into, the Russians took land from Germany and imposed a political framework on it (the battles on the Eastern front had been by far the most bloody and Russian anger can be justified, alas they were not at Versailles), this time the rest of the Allies did not impose as framework, rather allowed Germany to develop its own democracy. The result of all of this is that whilst Russia showed sufficient respect to gain respect from the Germans, the Western Allies showed them more respect, did not expect much of them and as a result, when Germany reunified they became Western leaning.

Targets and Judgement in war and peace

Technology comes at a cost and often this needs to be justified. Using billions worth of machinery and blowing up empty desert with it with nothing of strategic (or testing) value will cause a political storm. Of course, no matter how poor their judgement, a leader will not allow this to happen. Failure tends to occur the other way in the name of targets. Targets can be human, physical (or abstract which are necessarily more qualitative). In the case of human targets counting quantity can become more important than the qualities that they are designed to achieve. In Vietnam the US used the concept of body count[3] to incentivise troops in battle but numerous groups of soldiers killed civilians to make up the number of bodies expected of them, whilst losing the quality of humanity so necessary to win over an enemy. In Afghanistan and Iraq human target counts of top enemy coordinators were more important than the families that were incidentally blown up (even at weddings) with the loss of local support that resulted. These monstrosities were not to lead to success because they showed no respect but tyranny. However the tyranny was not sufficient to put down the local people as was the case on the Banda islands.

The obsession with targets does not just relate to war, it relates to all form of monitoring because it is easier to judge by numbers than to look at the issues behind them. It has led people to be allowed to die in the UK healthcare system because the relevant figure was under target and resources were allocated for another measure that was over target even though that was not critical in the case of patients dying. Nevertheless, the targets took precedence over human life because middle management were more focused on their targets than the doctors were on life. Judgement is crucial and no intermediate target should be the end, no matter how seduced by numbers we become, but all too often intermediate targets are the end. Many know the price of a bomb, many fewer the value and occasionally somebody appears in history like Alexander The Great who has no need for statisticians, he just wins wars.

Respect

In 1997, the US decided to engage with the Afghan Taleban rulers for the destruction of their opium crops because they were factories for drugs and in 2001 paid them for this work[4]. Then in the same year, after the Twin Towers massacre, the US decided to overthrow the Taleban for harbouring the terrorists.

Once in Afghanistan NATO changed the terms and stopped paying for the opium. It does not matter if this was because it was a new president's policy or if it was because of the invasion, it sequenced with the invasion and so any propagandist could use this to give the impression that withdrawal of monies was due to the invasion. The terms had changed from before, in the eyes of the farmers because NATO had a bit of power in Afghanistan.

In the harvest of May 2001, Opium production had fallen sharply compared to previous years, but by May 2002 when the Allies were in Afghanistan, production rose to near peak levels, to rise to new records within a few years[5,6].

Opium crops have increased which Russia feels the brunt of very heavily in deaths through heroin and Allied introduced pomegranate crops are being destroyed to be replaced by more Opium fields in Afghanistan, with the resulting drugs bought by the Taliban. Indeed, the 'neutral' Iranians found themselves in a position where they could accuse the NATO allies of charging Afghan farmers tax for the opium crop[7,8].

Whatever the conflicting reports, the Taleban are now using the opium trade to both make money from the farmers for weapons and give money to the farmers to get their loyalty. Whatever the situation now on alternative crops, like pomegranates the lot of ordinary farmers was hindered extremely by the invasion, and monies they were getting from the US stopped. Things had gotten worse for farmers, but the Taliban could still offer them money for their crops.

An anarchist prince engaging with any issues of war would do well to realise that you do not make peoples' lots worse as a result of your presence or destroy their crops, or markets. NATO have made clear they would not destroy the crops, but instead got rid of the markets[9]. Even an invading force needs some hospitality, and that requires goodwill, not punishment. It is better to punish directing minds than people who are just trying to make a living and have had no real say in any of the issues. Respect is as much about not punishing people who are not involved in an atrocity as punishing those that are.

As an aside, culturally the part of the world that Afghanistan is part of is part of a broader religion, Islam. The invasion of Iraq in 2003 was seen as unjust in that area, and the countries despite their differences are brothers through Islam. This second war gave a pattern of Islam being attacked and that lack of respect for peoples' religion as well as for their livelihoods was disastrous. When livelihoods get lost, people are known to look for a greater meaning, and religion provides this. However, if you attack peoples' livelihoods (by removing markets for goods) as well as attacking their religion and they then see people of their own religion end up buying their goods, it is very difficult for these people to see you respecting them. In fact they will think that you are trying to destroy them both materially and spiritually, and if you place people on this perceived death ground, they will inevitably fight against you all the harder.

Chapter 13: Moral Cases For War

This chapter aims to get the reader to understand how precise the reasons for sending in troops need to be.

Internal Disputes and practicalities

When police enter a violent domestic dispute, they only do so reluctantly. The reason for this is that the husband and wife can easily reform an alliance and attack the policemen or women called in to help. The same is true of large scale tribal differences in countries, outsiders are all too easily distrusted for meddling. In 1992 the US entered Somalia which was having internal troubles at the time The US entered initially on humanitarian grounds due to hundreds of thousands in danger of starving to death but before long they allowed themselves to be drawn into disputes and made the fatal mistake of trying to bring in their own solution through 'nation building[1,2].'

 The Serbians ha They were seen as meddling and (subtly) trying to 'tell' the Somalis what to do, were promptly attacked and soon found themselves leaving their humanitarian mission for their own safety and lack of desire to start a large scale dispute with Somalia, they had only been saving lives after all. What had started as a mission based entirely on good will ended up a disaster because warring groups with a common national bond are prone to take it out on the outsiders in the situation.

The liberation of Kosovo was achieved not just through violence but also diplomacy. Serbia was stable again following the collapse of Yugoslavia, and instead of tribes attacking each other there was a government systematically killing Kosovan Muslims. When the bombing of Sarajevo started (to try to force the Serbians to respect Kosovan space) it became apparent that Serbia would have to allow the protection of the Kosovans, free an airport for NATO but the Serbs themselves would not be 'told' what to do. The Russians stabilised the situation, as an old ally of Serbia, by taking control of the airport and 'allowing' NATO to use it, to Serbian outbursts of Joy.

 d not bowed to NATO who had used violence against them, rather they had trusted their old friend, Russia. Russia then allowed NATO troops in but there was a feeling in Serbia that they had secured a victory, whilst NATO had secured their objectives in relation to Muslim safety.

Northern Ireland and indeed Ireland have had a long and troubled history after England invaded in the 13th Century under the Papal Banner (as it had itself been invaded two hundred years before under the same banner by the same Normans). In the 1990's a peace process started that was entirely peaceful due to a number of dynamics combined with the overwhelming desire to get out of the violence that had overtaken any normal life (both sides had concluded that they could not win). The British and Irish governments forged a united front so that both the Unionist and Nationalist communities had the confidence to engage. The US government as both an ally of the IRA and the UK was able to work in a high profile manner, especially through Clinton giving both sides the 'feel good' factor. The result of all of this was that through this international diplomatic approach no one in Northern Ireland felt they were being told, they had either the British or Irish, and US government was on their side regardless. The deal that they sold was that, but without foreign help and the desire for peace, this could not have been achieved.

These examples point to a number of things, if tribes in a country go to war, keep out and if you must give food, you may need to resort to airdrop: The militias may get most of the food, but they will at least not be ransacking farms, rather potentially distributing an amount for propaganda purposes and feeding themselves before they kill each other, not the suppliers of the food (farmer or humanitarian worker). If a government is engaging in genocide, you can with difficulty stop that because you are fighting one, not two or more (tribes). The world will possibly never be totally free of genocide for good because humans are very good at manufacturing differences even where there really are none (for example football rivalries in the same city) but when parties are fed up of war, very careful diplomatic work needs more than one grouping to achieve it because the divided groups need to see divisions between the peace talkers, even if not in relation to the warring groups themselves, to take sides and not 'be told.' The idea that genocide is an excuse for military intervention can only hold true if there is one (directing) government who can have safe ground demanded of them. (With militias, this means all parties willing to offer neutral safe ground for reasons of territory). It is very rare that the carnage of regime change will be justified unless the slaughter is of the population proportions of the Killing Fields and Pol Pot, but this is a matter of judgement: Despite his brutality for many years the use of regime change to remove Saddam Hussein was not readily accepted in Iraq as was shown by the fallout of the Second Gulf War.

Invasion and the only reason for regime change

The UN allows people to go to war for reasons of mutual self defence against invasion and implemented attack, but the Gulf Wars showed with invasion how this must go further than just releasing annexed parties, rather removal of the leadership of the aggressor state itself. When Kuwait was invaded the UN formed a formidable alliance to remove Iraq from it. The armies did release Kuwait, did enter Iraq but decided against invasion rather imposing no flight zones[3] because they were afraid of splitting the coalition, particularly the Muslim parts and were afraid of a long bitter occupation[4].

This was to prove fatal, not only because Iraqis would have accepted regime change as demonstrated by the uprising of the Shia community in 1991 where over 60,000[5] were slaughtered, and also the Kurdish Community who also rose up and required safe havens from Saddam Hussein[6]. Saddam went about rebuilding his country and persecuting anyone who he considered a threat, but his presence on the international stage did not go and the ill feeling towards him grew. In the Second Gulf War, Saddam had done nothing new to instigate invasion but the British and US governments contrived to bombard accusations that could not be proved but built up the necessary hysteria to allow a totally unjustifiable war. The result was a fiasco, whether the planning for after hostility had been done or not, what was done totally underestimated the feelings of Iraqis and the fact that Saddam had prepared for this with a high ground, he had invaded no one this time. The resulting mess led to hundreds of thousands of lives lost, the Allies not being accepted and perversely the very Muslim Coalition that the Allies had been afraid to break in the first Gulf War, had now been destroyed to such an extent that some young British Muslims were willing to blow up their own countrymen and women[7].

It is better to lose some allegiance when your cause good, than try to demand it when your cause is bad. The example of Iraq should stand as proof that if the UN invade competently following an aggressor invasion you will be accepted, whereas without large percentages of the population being culled or their leader's invasion of another state, you will not be accepted. (In Afghanistan following their terror acts in 2001, we were accepted until we were seen to have changed the initial terms of engagement as discussed above). It was the failure to follow through the first gulf war that led directly to the second gulf war and haemorrhaging of Muslim support for the West. Afghanistan merely shows that if a country accepts an invasion because of the violence emanating from it, and the terms of the mission change in relation to the locals, so do the mindsets of the locals.

Nuclear Powers and Diplomacy

The stated case for regime change does imply invasion, but with some states (such as those with nuclear capabilities) full invasion would almost necessarily imply a nuclear holocaust. Understanding the mindsets of the generals in such a nation is critical in applying pressure to the body politic to remove at least those responsible from power, even if any following war crimes trial is entirely domestic. If a nation suffers the humiliation of partial invasion and the generals are against matters going any further, the plot of land invaded would become a symbolic issue that could be used to effect sufficient regime change so as to ensure that the issue at hand did not occur again very soon. If the country's generals were entirely behind the leader this course of action would be wreck less in relation to nuclear war so it would take diplomacy and judgement to know their state of mind.

A leader who loses domestic land to outsiders is placed in a very weak position politically and any advances into a country would have to increase the size of area controlled slowly enough to take account of the speed of political movement for fear of inciting the pride of the locals. If the locals and generals accept the invasion, the leader quickly loses her job. If the locals or generals incite the situation can easily tip into nuclear war. If neither locals nor generals are incited but the invasion is not accepted by both, the plot of land invaded would lead to the leader sufficiently nursing their wounds to not try aggression again Further when he was out of power negotiations (including global nuclear arms reductions) could easily follow over the handing back of the symbolic land.

The ultimate premise behind this section is that if someone takes something off someone, but they end up having to give that back and lose a little more in return, it is in the metaphor, not life and death (nuclear), just very embarrassing, and people do learn. Countries will fight to the death on the fear of destruction, but will blame their leaders if they are 'brought to their knees,' ie lose a bit of land for a short while.

Chapter 14: Lobbying

This chapter aims to show that lobbying will always exist and the reader had better be damn careful when engaging with it.

The need for consultation

Every government will enact laws. Every law can have intended effects but also unintended effects which can be both positive and negative. Every person has their own perspective and no person can be depended upon to see the perspectives of all others. In order to both avoid negative unintended effects and potentially exploit positive unintended effects, a government has to consult with people that the laws will either effect and the people that worry about the law's potential effects. This is the process of lobbying. It is essential for the smooth passage of policy to law, even if nothing in the legislation changes, as it is also about making people feel part of a process that effects them.

The problem with lobbying is the same as the problem with politics 'he who shouts loudest,' and in the case of lobbying, he who pays most. The corruption in this is best demonstrated by people who donate money to more than one party so whoever gets power, the winning party has to acknowledge and to a degree pay back in kind the monies that were paid to them. This is a way of vested interests putting a stranglehold on political parties. However individual politicians can still make their own judgements.

Gifts and being in someone's gift

Doctors in Britain get gifts from pharmaceutical companies, with all respect to the good faith of the medical profession, these companies have calculated that it affects sales of their products. Politicians are notoriously more corrupt than doctors and are prone to seek gifts for asking questions that can effect policy in the British Houses of Parliament both the House of Lords[1] and The House of Commons[2] being recent examples. Indeed recently fraudulent expenses show a mindset amongst our law makers that make the people who are caught taking money look more like the unlucky ones than the minority[3].

 It does not help that corrupt politicians mainly only have to apologise to their (in many cases corrupt) peers as a sanction, normally they will look after their fraternity and carry on with their ways. Of course people have eyes and politicians who take no gifts are not trusted ('You can't trust a man without a price' being a popular corrupt saying, whereas of course the opposite is true to the non corrupt), and to remain trusted you need to take gifts without being in someone's gift. For reasons of independence an anarchist prince must not allow himself to be bought or the corruptions of money win. Thomas More worked a way around this, he gave back gifts of similar or greater value[4] and kept to his principles to the point where his religious beliefs had him executed. However he was so trusted by his boss, King Henry VIII (who had him executed for his religious beliefs) that he famously commuted More's execution from disembowelment to beheading for brevity to lessen the pain, such was his regard for More[5].

Now politicians have a register of interests, but the corrupt will find a way through this so this chapter is not about the latest way of catching the corrupt out as these ways will change, likely like scissors, paper, stone.

The anarchist prince has to support those who get the team (party) funds without associating with them too closely. It is important to realise that you need these people in your team, finances are imperative in modern democracies, but it more important to realise that they work for the team. This chapter is just advice for an anarchist prince in staying clear of corruption which undermines all good intent. The easiest way is to avoid all fund raising but show respect to those in your team that do, pay for your own food, travel, accommodation and repay all gifts to the same monetary value: Payment in kind may start off as the easiest way but in the long run it is the curse of the corrupt.

Chapter 15: Markets and Who is in control

This aims to get any anarchist prince to relate to the wheels of money without losing their initial zeal.

Roles, Personnel, Excellence and Arrogance

To say that a person is making money in a company is not solely down to that person, it is the role that they are taking part in. If you are put in a position where you are selling cars, you are going to make less money than if you are selling high value financial products. It is the product that makes the money, the salesman who sells the product. It is often confused that the salesman is also the product, he is not. One example of people becoming so arrogant in their perceived excellence that they have lost the support of all society bar themselves are bankers who like to think that they are indispensable. They take bonuses when their company has run at a loss, to the point of insolvency, threatening to leave the company otherwise. In the financial meltdown of late 2000s they lost our taxpayers money and (and our people jobs as they had wrecked the lending money supplies), relied on our taxes to keep their own jobs and they still paid themselves bonus as essential for their 'excellence,' whilst threatening to leave the country if the top rate of tax went up to 50%. It was also noted that women in the banks performed better than their outspoken male colleagues, but there was no agenda put in place to stop the sexual discrimination to balance this. People who demand bonus when their banks are insolvent are a detriment to our society and mistake the excellence of the position that they are in with their own excellence. They had lost many people jobs at national minimum wage of just over £5 per hour but their million pound bonuses represented £480 per hour worked on top of their basic wage (assuming a 40 hour week 52 weeks a year). We will relate to levels of pay for highest and lowest earners later.

Product Standards need Ethical Human and Environmental Standards

The EU has a policy on freedom of the passage of goods that are up to various product standards[1]. For example, children's toys cannot have spikes that easily come out for fear of the child in the EU injuring themselves badly. However, companies can sell goods in the EU whether or not they are made by child slave labour in the third world or indeed without any regard to the environment. Companies have an attitude that politicians from various countries need to compete to get their investment in jobs in that country by lowering standards and taxes, but demand of the same politicians free access to their markets without restrictions through human and animal rights to the needs of the planet. It is a damnation on politicians who covet power so much that they do not use their markets to force these multinationals into standards not only on products sold, but also the treatment of the people and countries involved in making them. The anarchist prince will notice that legally they can exchange access for markets in return for good behaviour from companies but will also notice that the lobbying machine can easily turn on them very hard if they try this, not least by funding other parties.

The technological need for the concentration of capital

Many innovations that are useful for a society as a whole are driven by state funding, the computer to crack enemy codes, the world wide web to communicate and retain information in the case of global nuclear meltdown. However, these basic versions did not do much to improve the quality of individual lives tangibly until individuals and so private companies got involved to give us products with 'creature comforts.'

As companies grow they generate (in good conditions) increasing profits. These profits are used amongst other things, to pay tax, bonus, shareholders dividends, to repay debts and fund the research of new products. A company that mass produces technologies concentrates the monies of all the people who buy them. If a product costs 1 currency unit to produce, is sold at the factory gate for 3 units and a million of these products are sold, a million people pay a handful of units but the company makes 2 million of these currency units. This concentration of wealth allows companies to make ever more complex and intricate technologies which includes environmental technologies.

Company size, power, influence and corruption

The argument above indicates that a large company can push forward innovation, it can, but if a company becomes too large it can use its position to abuse the powers at its disposal, lobbying to the point of bribery, bullying producers of goods in oversized retailers (for example supermarkets not paying farmers enough to survive as they have total market dominance), even defying courts until their preferred politicians are put in power. Microsoft and their operating systems were being split off from their office (spreadsheet, word processor) operations during the US Clinton years. The US courts had tried to break up Microsoft in two because their success led to such a market position that it was stifling competition[2] as testified by its owner being the richest man in the world at the time. However, when George W Bush came to power, Microsoft were allowed off the hook.

It is easy for venture capitalists to split companies because they have the absolute power to do so, it is more difficult for politicians to do so because they fear that the opposing political party will be the grateful recipient of a large donation. This proves that venture capitalists have more power over business and the frameworks in which they operate than politicians who pride themselves on making the laws, albeit the ones that big businessmen will allow.

The need for distribution of monies and education

If capitalism concentrates monies, there needs to be a balance between these concentrations and the need for monies to reach all in a society. Trickledown economics is sited as generating wealth for the poorest parts of the country. However the timescale from William I taking all lands in Britain to the point where hunger was largely left wanting took until after even the effects of the Jarrow Marches[3], a period of nearly 900 years. Redistribution is one way to facilitate this but has potential flaws if money is given for nothing. This is not an argument for workfare, rather an observation that someone without a job will feel happy for a few weeks if their benefits go up, but will soon forget and remember the boredom of being on benefits. Extra money does not buy happiness, but reduction of money to the point where well being cannot be sustained will lead to misery. However, extra monies being paid for retraining has both the effect of the monies being earned, skills being learned, the economic talent pool being broadened and for the amounts and time involved, a sense of achievement but no sense of slave labour.

Discrepancies over pay within a company

Coming back to the excesses of bankers, and their claims of other people needing them, we can let them help up other peoples' wages which will help us all become for appreciative of the 'wealth creating' bankers. People working in capital intensive industries can earn far more than the national average of the country in which they operate. The main argument for them not to be taxed is that they have the wealth to easily move. There are many who would call their bluff, but setting absolute limits on a company's pay is likely to lead to resentment sufficient for people on principle to walk. It may be attractive to call peoples' bluff but is likely to be more destructive than productive, no one likes an arbitrary glass ceiling no matter how high it is set.

Another approach is to look at the lowest paid employee in a company (or working at that company's premises) and their wage split up into basic and bonus (pro rata) and total them. Instead of setting the top amount to pay at an absolute, it can be a multiple of this total over the lowest paid. These multiples would be set annually by the National Statistical Service based on data from the National Audit Office (because data needs quality as well as quantity) and if the top paid wanted more, they would have to pay the bottom more, and pecking orders would see to those in the middle consolidating their positions. This would be of benefit to a company, from top to bottom they would be able to attract higher and higher quality staff the more they paid whilst retaining a sense of social responsibility.

There is the consideration of people with short career lives, for reason of illness or even for being professional athletes. It would be easy to put any monies they earned a year over the maximum in a trust fund to pay for them later in life. If during their short career they worked for more than one organisation, they could have multiple trust funds with the ability to draw on only one at a time. The level of the top pay the organisation at that time would be the amount that they could draw, whether in the UK or abroad. If they did not use up all their monies in a lifetime, they could designate charities to benefit from the rest of these funds on their death.

On stopping international companies harming local communities

As individuals take to supermarkets, so do supermarkets fail to engage with the local community just offering a range of goods that are by no means exhaustive but are sufficiently large to put small community shops into peril[4]. Many small shops (retail and catering) help local environments as hubs of information and communication as well as selling specialised goods with specialised services. Huge supermarkets generate huge profits at the cost of the small community shop which simply does not have the buying power to compete with costs.

Currently in the UK a Supermarket and a Small Company pay two taxes, one based on floor space payable to the local authority and one based on profit payable to central government. It should be noted that another percentile of profit could be decided by and paid to the local authority to go directly into a fund based on the number of man hours spent and units of floor space in the local enterprise, in both cases weighted as a measure between units both of goods sold and of revenues gained through the tills to encourage tailor made as opposed to inhuman service. This fund could pay out based on number of employees, floor space, equally between company units or more likely a weighted average of these.

The balance of these measures in retail would need the measures including taxation weighting by each local authority by means of using pilots. With 400 authorities trying these schemes out, material of what works will quickly develop. If businesses say they get no profit from being in a community, an anarchist princess would tell them to leave that community and as business needs a market she would have called their bluff. Business tries to tell market controllers that they are more important than their customers. A watchdog television show that takes only the highest value cases will not tell you otherwise. An anarchist princess will see through this.

The Slavery Of Debt

Zero interest is an anti monetarist argument about debt (like zero economic growth where irreplaceable consumption would be a greater worry), but the result, in part because of inflation would lead to no one lending. Zero interest is very caring philosophically unless your family are starving.

The problem with the slavery of debt is best magnified when the poor have paid their debts off three times over but still owe more than they borrowed, with rates up to 90% a month. Debt analysis breaks into a number of areas, the debt, inflation, national interest rates, risk factors, loading factors, office costs and finally profit but one thing can remain universal despite someone's credit rating, how much they pay back in total as a percentage of the initial debt: For example, if an individual (assumed here in terms of the higher levels of inflation and national interest rates) has paid off double their initial debt in five years (equivalent 15% interest over inflation/interest rates per year), or has paid off triple in ten years (equivalent 12% interest p.a.) or quadruple in 15 (equivalent to 10% interest p.a.) and so on, then the book on their debt simply needs to shut. They have paid off more than enough. This is another example of monies over time. As a side note, if zero interest only allows friends of the rich to get money, our current system will keep the poor in permanent debt. Neither no interest nor unbridled interest are right, but our system caves in to one or another. The anarchist prince would do well to analyse debt, the numbers and engage with the two poles in this issue.

Why Cash is best

Because their job is to uphold the law, the police wish to shut down anything that is unlawful, whether the law is virtuous or not. They are already concerned with damning anyone who uses cash[5]. Cash is a medium of exchange that the banks cannot take from any individual or individuals, having the system working entirely by card gives the banks and state untold powers over our economic liberty.

Probability dictates that over time, a patronage based (party political) system will corrupt, and any political party that stands against such a state when this goes too far can be deemed illegal and have assets frozen and card payment units (the things that shopkeepers ask you to put your credit card in) blocked. If those political parties cannot collect cash, then all the liberties that the corrupted political class wish to take from them will be taken, likely with violence. If in this corrupt system, political parties that are deemed unfit by the state can collect the cash whilst deemed illegal then they will have the resources to mobilise and the political class will be forced to engage, likely with less violence.

It is important to note therefore that the passage of common understanding is not violent, but the closure of that passage is violent.

Capitalism needs cash, as do unauthorised bodies seeking representation even if against it. It is important for an anarchist princess to understand that the control of financial worth should not just lie with our banks and the cards they let us use, it should lie in our hands as cash to do with what we want, even if it does sometimes break the law as that is not always perfect either.

Chapter 16: Elites

This chapter aims to show that groups have structure and will lead to a number of subgroups forming the strongest knowledge and power base, which need to be accountable.

The need for elites

High level courts each have a judge. The judge may be elected or appointed, but in both cases must have the respect of a group of their peers to have a realistic hope of getting the position. This is important, two clients fight a case, criminal or civil, they each have representatives from the legal profession who have passed exams and therefore had a codified form of patronage. The judge may adjudicate, or a jury, but even then the judge passes sentence. The two lawyers are battling to set out two different interpretations of an alleged reality and lawyers being in a competitive situation are known to over step the mark. It is up to the judge to keep track of where these lawyers are going for his own sake, or the sake of a jury who are not expected to be legally trained. The judge has to keep control and is part of an elite that keep watch over the (often young) lawyers, the best of whom may in their own day join the elite of judges and fume at people making spurious arguments that they themselves once did. Judges are and need to be an elite, they need the wits and the legal skills to unpick the inevitable sophistry that arises during court cases. My proof of this is that if all judges by law were removed from a case and an extra untrained juror put in his place, there would be so many miscarriages of justice that the government implementing this would either back down and be totally humiliated and/or be thrown out at the next available juncture.

Of course the only elites are not judicial, lawyers are needed in the legislature as well as the technically proficient being represented (ideally in the legislature but more likely) the advisory bodies. Differing industries have their own elites, there are elites of people deemed to have the transferrable skills to move between industries. Politicians even though jockeying for position have their elites, there are educational, and medical elites and though this is not exhaustive, even anarchistic computer hackers have their own elites. The elites are ideally the top echelons of meritocracies that allow the most proficient to rise hit the coal face of knowledge and understanding and in turn help develop and guide the rest. The elite of the proletariat are all people from all groupings that have a vote when deciding their governments. Governments can pull the wool over the peoples' eyes once, but rarely twice.

How no individual is indispensible

'The higher you get, the harder you fall.' Though this may be true, it is also true that the more powerful the people that cover you the safer you are, unless the national media or the law get involved and covers get blown. The result of this is people in elites can start to think themselves as untouchable both because comparatively 'minor' failures and even tyrannies get overlooked and because these people realise that as a result they can get away with up to murder. One example of this followed the Second Gulf War, and a top government Scientist Dr Kelly in 2003 had questioned the validity of the government claims about Iraq's weapons of mass destruction[1]. The official story is that despite his good mental health, personal relationships and happy disposition that he went into the countryside and committed suicide. Very few British people believed this, rather to uphold government lies he was highly dispensable and was killed to protect the position on an illegal and immoral war.

However, dispensability does not only come from the top down, it comes from the bottom up. Margaret Thatcher believed that she was indispensable in her position as Conservative Party Leader to the extent when a potential vote on her was looming at the height of her (especially electoral) difficulties with the Community Charge which became 'a serious political problem[2].' The environment was such that one did challenge and she found out the hard way that she was perfectly dispensable, like the all the rest of us. Interestingly the challenger Michael Heseltine destroyed his own leadership chances by destroying hers[3].

The nature of dispensability in the media varies from high quality investigative journalism into corruption and abuse of power, to the quality of reporting around the religious views of a national football manager. Glenn Hoddle was English National Football manager, believed in reincarnation, and was asked if people could come back as a needing a wheelchair if they had led bad lives. Alas he was not theologian and replied 'yes,' rather than suggest a blade of grass. He was sacked as national manager for discrimination, because the English did not understood the religion he was referring to, nor he how to express it[4].

The moral of this is that your bosses can destroy you if you push too hard against their interests, your peers can if you push too hard at theirs, the media, law (even drink driving at just over the limit can lose people their jobs), and other elites can destroy you if you push too hard against them, or when very bad news hits the court of public opinion, it generally terminal. It is necessary for the Anarchist Prince therefore whilst ensuring their personal safety and legal position, to use position but not rely on it, for if the Anarchist Prince is worth anything at all, (s)he will upset interests.

How elites can be replaced

The French Revolution is probably the most drastic expression of an elite being replaced. Though the revolution started the concept of Secularism[5],

as a first of its kind it was remarkably bloody, at least until the fall of Robespierre. However, the French also managed to replace a king with an emperor (Napolean) as a result and went off to invade much of Europe. This was a far cry from the initial desire to escape poverty and starvation.

Revolutions since then have been more sophisticated, even if a whole group of people have to be killed, a power vacuum is deemed as dangerous. Instead of just having a people rise, there needed to be an elite ready to put in place to stop the unpredictability of a power vacuum. The Russian October Revolution was an example of this, though there was an ideological need to assassinate the entire Royal Family, including minors, but Lenin was clear that he needed to be in control, in effect he orchestrated a coup d'etat[6].

 The Velvet Revolution in Czechoslovakia was one step forward still, seen to be spontaneous, no one died and the government was replaced by Havel and his team. It turned out afterwards that people thought the whole process was spontaneous, but in fact many Czechs and Slovaks believe this was highly orchestrated[7,8]. However, a revolution with popular support and without bloodshed can only be called a success, conspiracy or not.

Such revolutions happen in most countries now in the form of elections, they are codified forms of revolution or (if the incumbent is successful) attempted revolution, without bloodshed unless it is a disastrous election. In most countries the choice is between two established main parties, with peripheral parties taking part in some countries also. The established parties can become complacent but then they lose vote. If they know that there is no third party snapping at their heels, they can rest in a comfort zone of not updating, not challenging for power but this will not last forever. However, it does lead to the corruption of the party in power (as they cannot see themselves losing vote such is the state of their opposition) and so the country at large. An anarchist prince needs to realise that if there are not people constantly reforming all the main parties, the ideal of revolution by election gets replaced with stagnation, corruption and a body politic that is not dealing with current reality, and then dangerous revolutionary forces can easily start to come to the fore.

Chapter 17: On threats to the state and the state being a threat

This chapter aims to show that politicians with all their excesses need to be controlled as well as the people.

Why politicians need to be controlled

From the Norman invasion when the English government was set up to be Feudal, a king was accountable to his barons, indeed the Barons needed to accept a King (they could not accept Queen Matilda[1]), stay loyal but could act rebelliously or violently against the monarch if they felt the monarch was not upholding his side of the bargain(King John and Edward II found out what happened when the Barons played up and in the latter case paid for it with his life). The central point of Feudalism was society was divided into ranks and every rank had to be loyal to the next rank up or down as was appropriate. This was seen as a way of controlling people in their positions. It was archaic but to a fair degree it worked. Though until Magna Carta, a King could slaughter his own people in a raid on any town, after they had to allow people to be tried by their peers before the removal of privileges, liberties or life[2].

The danger had been reduced from monarchs slaughtering innocents in their own country to slaughtering innocents in a different country, which if progress was certainly very subtle intellectually if not physically.

Power has transferred step by step from the King, to Parliament (where the Barons sat) which gained a lot more control through the Tudors, who used acts of parliament to control the Barons, but parliament gained an ascendancy which combined with a power crazed monarch (Charles I) determined to put parliament down caused the Civil War leading to the Parliamentary Protectorate[3], Monarchs returned with less powers and whilst the first King, Charles II was very popular, James II caused troubles by seeking to appoint Catholics into top positions (which with England having a fiercely Protestant Parliament) led to his downfall, and the result was a further clipping of the wings of the monarch. The glorious Revolution in 1688 caused King James II to flee the country with Parliament responding the Triennial Act[4]. Amongst other things, The Trennial act took gave parliaments fixed terms and judges immunity from the King. However, the ordinary man was still not represented and this was to take around 150 years to start to change.

From a base of your vote towards parliament being based on amount of land you owned, the Great Reform Act of 1832 started the movement to one man one vote but still only the property owning group voted[5], in 1867 these rights were extended to most in towns and some in rural areas[6], and in

1884 rural areas were addressed and things got closer still to one man one vote, though women were still totally excluded[7]. It would take some more decades for women to get the vote, 1918 would see the wealthier ones and 1928 would see it extended to all women over 21[8].

The pattern that these events follow is simple, an unaccountable monarch followed by an unaccountable parliament followed by the wealthier people being politically unaccountable in their votes leading to a full electorate being unaccountable in its decisions. The trend has been from one to a few to the many, power is dissipated at election time when people vote, it stays compressed in the leadership during the period of a government. As no one could question the King's will once, no one legally can question the will of the people (Note this only applies to UK law, other laws may be different, Afghanistan[9] and Iran[10] 2008 through corruption rigged votes and more interestingly the US in 2000 decided 'legally' that some votes could not be counted[11]).

The world has arguably become safer since power has dissipated which may have to do with power in the hands of the many leaving those in government with less power and so less a tendency to become corrupt. However power still impacts on judgement: an individual may like an idea that is totally insane (even though with most thoughts (s)he has may be very wise), but many people will know someone who questions such 'insane' ideas. This is why decisions need to be verified by more than just one person. Though leaders can still destroy and voting bodies can behave like herds, trying to pull over a large body of people who are not power corrupted to something totally unreasonable is much more difficult than to win over a power crazed individual. This is why politicians need controlling by the many. It should be noted that Nazi Germany is an example where a fledgling democracy was pulled into insanity by people following one man, but most mature and so more stable democracies steer clear of the philosophy of simply destroying everything that is inconvenient.

Politicians without our vote have too much power, politicians with our vote kill in our name. They may say it is killing in the name justice, but it is body politic's interpretation of justice and so ultimately politicians that are killing in our name (having elected them as an electorate if not individually) that smears the blood on our hands which puts us in peril. They are our elected dictators, with the powers of a king between them, with all the potential corruption and destruction that that entails. They are also not necessarily virtuous and, some rumour, have control over an individual's social, political, and financial status: Gordon Brown, before he was even UK Prime Minister was considered by his Tony Blair to be 'mad, bad and dangerous beyond redemption,' that he 'had something wrong with him,' and that he was 'flawed, lacking perspective and having a paranoia about him[12]. Fear of power can drive politics and if the person at the top has a personality disorder, party loyalties will cover up 'indiscretions,' as once again the death of Dr Kelly indicates. Just being in a democracy is no real protection to vested interests should they become powerful enough. The best way for an anarchist prince to stay safe from politicians is to not bother with them, but getting involved in politics at some point, alas, means having to deal with those in power, good, bad or ugly.

Why politicians control

Unfortunately, human constructs for the distribution of power are basic, we take orders, compete on the same level and give orders. The competition is to work out who gives or takes more amongst peers. We need a single power at the top, two separate groups will often compete for power without recourse to legality as insurrections (against Apartheid) or Civil War show. Even with the separation of powers, everything done by our military, judiciary, royalty, legislature is done in the name of the country, the people with other nominal titles to give the appearance (and often reality) of virtuosity. Even the media, who are ultimately the only private sector part of our constitutional checks and run for profit, may need to justify their behaviour in the national interest (even when being bipartisan) when they communicate about affairs of the state.

However, someone must be in control of all of this and act as a directing mind, both because someone has to deal with the overall picture and also as troop animals, we need to feel that someone is in control. Even Communism with all its relating to equality, in every instantiation has required a leader to be recognised by all in the country. We need to feel that we have an ultimate watchman and some degree of feeling about our ultimate watchman, if we are at all politically aware, whatever the system.

This control can mobilise a great number of people to do a great number of things, from war to health systems to secret services to tax to benefits to business development to defining crime. However, most politicians do not change social attitudes as much as they would like to.

For all political excesses, we still trust people with power, and this lack of learning from tyranny proves that it is instinctive that we organise ourselves in power structures because we can achieve more together than alone. This is the ultimate reason why we let someone control, they can do much good for us, but they can potentially destroy us too. We can try to remove politicians that are failing but may not always be able to, immediately or whilst they are alive.

Why war and tyranny start from people out of control

In 1982 Argentina invaded the Falklands as they had a historical claim to it[13]. That was the stated reason. The reality was the Argentine economy was failing, and Galtieri was the third dictator in six years and decided a symbolic foreign policy victory was what he needed to secure his position[14]. He failed to notice that the British Prime Minister was in a terrible situation in her own opinion polls, she had the lowest rating of any UK Prime Minister in history[15] and he decided to invade the Falkland Islands. The UK's Thatcher saw an excuse to have her own opinion poll boost and engaged in a war over the Islands. She won, he lost, she won the next election in 1983 with ease, he lost power, was convicted of negligence and imprisoned[16].

As for Tyranny, In Tiananmen square, Iran, Iraq, Zimbabwe, Russia, UK and many other countries beside leaders that have feared for their control over power and have resorted to acts of violence because they are no longer loved and therefore feel the need to be feared. At this point they are out of control.

Ultimately it is the inability to let go of power is what makes politicians lose control, some are evil, those that engage in war and tyranny, but most are human and that concentration of power will corrupt even the best to a degree. The best way to avoid war and tyranny is to have accountable leaders and to ensure every leader can be removed through stable and difficult mechanisms outside of election time, as is the case with most party politics: Even if a general election is not called, a party can sort out its own affairs with its representation guaranteed until the next election. It should be noted though these systems are also capable of atrocities, though generally to a lesser degree. In writing this, I do not consider Bush elected as US leader at the time of the second gulf war, though for my country's grief, our Prime Minister Blair had to back him in the invasion of Iraq, and although Blair's party did not stop the war, they got rid of Blair for it, four years later. This is about as accountable as our leaders are now, he still won a general election after the invasion because his opponents had the image of being a laughing stock only interested in talking about immigration. Few on the British left like Blair, let alone want to follow in his footsteps, but most voted for him in the election following the invasion because whatever they felt about that, the alternative from the Conservatives was to them worse. Therefore not even a democracy can guarantee a country to not behave like tyrants, though a strong opposition in a democracy can help.

There is a moral in this, following Iraq in the subsequent 2005 UK elections The Conservatives were associated with the potential killing of 10,000 British through cold winters, lack of heating, and Health Care cuts. Labour were involved in actually killing many more than this, but these people were Iraqis, not British. Which tyranny did our left vote for? The reality of murdering many innocents abroad (Iraq) instead of the worry of less being killed domestically (Conservatives) because tyranny many can accept, as long as it is not too close to home.

Chapter 18: On Chimpanzees

This chapter aims to get the reader to see us in our chimpanzee anthropological context and how for unity we need to work through the troop structure.

Fusion Fission

Nature has a way of dealing with things and it is not by maintaining a permanent optimum constant, rather trying to maintain an optimal range. Using the case of blood sugars, when blood sugars are high, insulin release is stimulated which in turn lowers blood sugar, this lower level of sugar in turn inhibits the release of insulin and increases the release of glucagon (to stimulate the increase of blood sugars pulled from bodily reserves), and once the level is too high again insulin is released once more and glucagon inhibited. This is a very simple method used by nature by looking at an optimum, deciding if you're too low, or too high and acting. This system evolved with vertebrates, is hundreds of millions of years old and has still not perfected a way of being in a permanently optimal state when dealing with one chemical glucose (or blood sugar). Instead it uses negative feedback to keep blood sugars within a range of the optimum levels required for life.

Behaviour is inherently more complicated, with each human (or chimpanzee) having various characteristics, patience, aggression, sense of fun amongst other things and if the conclusion of these characteristics were at all possible to hold into a static calm state, an optimum mood, then holding blood sugar levels at an optimum would have been achieved many millions of years ago.

Unsurprisingly the main chimpanzee group behaviour breaks into two main phases, fusion, where the troop (or group) stays and works very closely together, and fission where individuals split up and have their own space and time instead of violence[1]. There is not one state that is optimal for the group, rather two which allow different qualities to show at different times and like blood sugars have a negative feedback system around them, too long apart and the Chimps want to come back together, too long together and the Chimps want to be on their own again. In human terms, there are times when the chimpanzee is individualistic and other times when she is communally based.

It is interesting that chimpanzees can be tribal between groups, but humans can also between states: The right wing in politics traditionally stands for the individual, the left wing traditionally stand for the commune and the voting public exercises a negative feedback between the two, when the leadership goes too far one way, the public sends them the other, and once that's gone too far, the electorate swings back again, just like the biological systems around blood sugar.

Blood sugar teaches us that as biological beings, negative feedback systems are inevitable. The size of our states now are not small chimpanzee troops of a couple of dozen individuals. Fusion fission teaches us that individualistic (right) or communal (left) politics are inevitable. Neither is right or wrong intrinsically, rather may be the right or the wrong approach given the situation (within the context of biological feedback). Most on the right can relate to some on the left and vice versa because neither position is unnatural yet neither eternally optimal.

Troops, hats and power sets

Troops: The troop structure is something that pervades human behaviour, in any situation we like to know who is in charge, some like even more to be in charge. The person in charge has a team who under most circumstances will try to display loyalty. People like to have confidence in the structure, do as they are told if it is not too unreasonable (in the main) and they have a sense of identity with that troop. The same is the structure of a chimpanzee troop, there is a chimpanzee in charge, and mostly the others are loyal, with others plotting their day when they will be in charge. Human troops represent themselves in a variety of ways, from the golf club structure to the structure of government. A government through its leader has relationships with leaders of other governments in the name of our country and modifies its relationships, themselves laid down by successions of leaders interactions with others. It should be noted that there is no necessary imperative for the leader of the government (or golf club) to care about people outside their circle as long as they can retain power without those people.

Hats: Humans are of course more complex than chimpanzees in terms of consciousness and level of tool manipulation, whereas chimpanzees may eat various fruits and starches, we have farmers who grow each of these various fruits. The farmers have joint 'hats:' Farmer, but have different hats for each of the types of fruit grown, a citrus fruit farmer, a grain farmer, each with different skills and knowledge bases but often similar distribution networks that they have to deal with. They all have an interest in how the group behaviour of 'the customer' (another hat that we all share at some point in the week) is affecting their livelihoods, under the hat of the type of farmer that they are. However, these farmers will also have hats of political identity, national identity and identities through their spare time activities. Hats mean people have things in common. Competitions between people within particular hats this leads to rivalries within the group. However, when people meet in a different place (like fruit farmers at an automobile show) this leads to common interests, rapports and so to connections ('oh, you work in that as well, wow!') between people in abstract troops through their abstract hats, or in modern terms, we have societies within society.

Power sets: Consider a set of two hats, car owner (with the licensing authority being in charge) and local golf club (run by the committee). An individual may have interest in none, either one or both. This choice is the power set of cars and golf. With three interests, cars, golf and choir singing, someone may be interested in none, any one of the three, any two of the three or all three. The more interests say N in total, the number of power set choices one person has is 2^N which in relation to the range of human interests makes the power sets incalculable. The proof of this is simple, suppose we have M people and N potential interests then the total possibilities available for each person with each choice of interests is 2^{MN}, so if we have 10 interests on offer and 10 people, maths aside the choice of combinations of people and interests is staggeringly over 10 billion billion billion.

As this is a fraction of population size of and interest choice within humanity, it makes these combinations totally incalculable.

Power sets should be used not to try to calculate anything here, but to appreciate we are more than just the car driver, the tax payer or the golfer we have interests in a great many things.

Bringing the three together: We operate as troops, but we all belong to more than one troop through hats, we have identities within these troops through the sides they bring out of us but cannot deal with this numerically, the number of options are incalculable. However, it does lead to a concept.

One Nation

We all have many different interests and to a degree, everyone lives in their own world and in an ever more differentiated society everyone needs shared hats to keep some identity with each other through troop behaviour in relation to our society. When a war arises, the national ego becomes strong and when a country consider their contribution to be for the good, this unites people very strongly. In peace time we become more partisan, especially politically. As a troop we need to be able to unify, and better in anticipation of troubles rather than waiting for them to happen. We need a common identity to stop the permissiveness of one political party raping one interest group and another, and, well, another. The UK Conservative Party coined One Nation politics in the 19th century [2], UK Labour took it on board in the 20th century[3] but there is still some way to go. Neither side recognises that the other believes in this concept and in a society moving further and further away from a unifying war (WWII) people grow ever more distrustful of parliamentarians more interested in lining their nests than representing anyone. 'I disagree with every word you say, but would die for your right to say it' may have been true in 1945, it is not true in the UK in 2009 and that is where if Britain's troop does not find a common identity somewhere, the division will allow for such sequential destruction or the poor destroying the rich and then the rich destroying the poor as to render our dreams of progress meaningless.

Leaders acting for one nation will simply seek to represent those that did not vote for them as well as those who did. Just because some politicians do not give a damn about this ideal, does not mean that it is wise to follow in their footsteps and give up on the concept, rather root them out and have them replaced.

Two or more Nations in One and The Holocaust

The alternative to one nation is a country being split into two or more. There have been quasi theories that if a leader looks after two thirds of the population and lets one third sink, that leader will stay in power. Making a group of people 'good' and a minority 'bad' gives people moral excuse to treat the 'bad' people in a way that is unimaginable. In Africa following the end of colonisation, many tribes were split between countries and countries between tribes. The resulting violence, rape and murder from the civil wars that followed was for one reason, the countries were two or more nation countries. Hitler took this to the extreme by totally ostracising the Jews in his country and history tells us the rest.

There is a lesson in this for the Anarchist Prince, if through bitter experience (s)he is disillusioned with politicians failing to act for One Nation, and wishes to give up on the concept altogether, then (s)he should take one long hard look at the alternative and a disintegrating society. Yes, politicians could put chemicals into non selected people's water to reduce their breeding (that is non selected people by the politicians), but on examination there was fear of the people involved finding out[4].

Chapter 19: One World Government

This chapter aims to impress the dangers of too much power for politicians through scale of the state, yet the need to have unifying global concepts.

The dangers of only one governmental space

The biggest argument for one world government is to stop war. There are also more flippant arguments like ensuring the super rich cannot play off countries in their tax rates in a bid to avoid paying it. The tax argument probably cannot be countered directly, but war can and indirectly through it tax.

If we have one world government, it is fair to assume that on its creation there would be a unifying figure of the like of Nelson Mandela as he so successfully achieved in South Africa followed by a period of virtuous government. However two forces would be at play, first corruption because of the scale of the venture and power bequeathed to the central controlling force, leading to dangers to liberty. Second the ability of humans to agree to a compromise leader without much virtuosity, and the resulting dangers to liberty there. Every Plan A needs a Plan B should plan A fail, and when (as would become inevitable probabilistically over time) a leader who started to oppress freedom corruptly, there would be no place left on earth for dissidents, Plan B and the platforms they would need to generate popular debate would disappear. Indeed when Yeltsin was defending the Russian Parliament from the Communist Generals' coup attempt, the communications link to outside Pro Democracy countries and their television sets was deemed as one major factor in Yeltsin's tactics, the plotters had cut off Gorbachev's communications, but the soldiers would not shoot their own people and cut off Yeltsin's, and the media glare probably had an impact on that[1]. If there had been no outside force to at least bring shame upon the Generals, Russia's developing democracy could and probably would have died as just that, the communist generals would have not had to even blush at anyone. As we learned in replacing elites, a new elite needs to be ready to put in place to stop disintegration like in the French Revolution. However, in a one world tyranny these activists, that would be the next elite, would have to be scattered for safety without a safe place to join forces to politically move. This is because they would be living in the knowledge that if they caught together, they would all die and the uprising would need to start all over again. But scattering their forces overly would render them totally ineffective. This would make joint communication impossible on the time scales required in revolutionary politics and would mean that any government taking away freedom would be able to ensure that no one rose against them.

Europe's response to Hitler and its lessons

Hitler amassed a huge army on coming to power. He started a horror of a war and after it was all over Europe resolved that this must not happen again. The first point that was identified in the peacetime period was that Germany had had too much coal and steel, the basis of any armament process. Six Countries signed the European Coal and Steel Community (ECSC) to keep a track on the trade on these substances by a 'high authority' as trade was seen as a way of keeping peace[2]. So far, so good, then it fell apart. The signing of the European Economic Community Treaty (EEC) made the false Machiavellian premise that 'ever closer union' meant total Union because of the seeking of supranational political union, rather than merely looking for cooperation[3].

The fear, under Machiavellian political rules was the alternative to getting ever closer was to get further apart. They did not see the possibility of the two forces antagonistically playing over time, some bonds getting weaker of time, new bonds replacing them. With ECSC the determination would be to cooperate in new areas even if some old areas became defunct (in the same way as a married couple work to keep their marriage together by reinforcing bonds, doing new things to act as one even though they always remain two separate people in relation to their rights and egos). Instead the EEC was a determination to concentrate power to the centre again. In 1992 the Treaty of Maastricht ensured an aim towards common foreign policy, which if ever achieved would effectively mean that every country would have to do as they were told by the European Foreign Minister in all of their dealings with the outside world[4]. Hitler had shown (as many others before him in Europe dating back to pre history) that one grouping of people who are too powerful have a leader far too powerful with all the corruption and war mongering that that opens. The European Union has already had high level scandals at the top to the extent that the entire Commission (which it should be noted was completely cross party as well as cross nation) has had to resign[5] before we are even at political union. European Countries (well once again politicians) had made the mistake of following in Hitler's footsteps on power with the belief that it needs ever more concentration, yet in most of these European Countries they try to both centralise and devolve power within their nation. On a European level there is only the tendency to centralise power. This contradiction between their internal and external politics has led to a Europe that is known for being too powerful in relation to the nation state and known for being a corrupt a one way street where individual countries will easily lose their right to govern themselves. An Anarchist Prince would do well understand that power cannot be disseminated amongst us all if we pursue structures with ever more power like continental powers (European Union) or even World Government.

On why religious humility needs more than one religion

After the Protestant Reformation leading to a break with The Pope's dominion, England was attacked by a Spanish Armada in 1588.

If Rome or Spain whichever you choose had won, the English would have been subjected to torture on an ecclesiastical scale, and many would have been burned alive for heresy (being a Protestant), as had been under the rule of England's Catholic 'Bloody' Mary (Queen Mary I).

The first time (after the Roman Empire) the Roman Church came to England, it was with humility and an attitude of persuasion because the church was humble and seeking to spread without force[6]. At the time of the Armada, barring the early Protestant revolution, the Roman Church was the only real religious force in Western Europe. It was corrupt to the point of having three Popes at once[7] whilst burning non Catholics into submission (including potentially anyone who disagreed with any of the teachings of the church, even without foundation in The Bible[8]). This is not a critique on the assumptions of The Roman Church, rather an observation that with too much power the assumptions of a church can go tragically wrong. One World religion is as dangerous as One World government, because the apparatus of a faith is a network that can do as much damage as the apparatus of a state. It should be noted that state and church can damage one another, but also help one another. Religion is about helping the acceptable towards the ideals and politics is about making reality something acceptable. Leaders in both need to be humble, not corrupt and the concentration of power directly affects these attitudes as no matter what hat is worn, power is power and highly corrupting.

One World Hat

In the same way as the One Nation hat cannot be fully enforced in a legal system, a One World hat if properly constructed would lead to deeper understanding of shared responsibilities without the need for world government. There are aspects to this hat, environmental, military, cultural, religious but can be achieved by agreement leading to a deeper understanding of ourselves and each other. Like the car driver having an interest in road issues, a planet driver (each and every one of us) has an interest in our Earth. Deals have and can be done through the UN, currently because of the finances involved, Environmental Treaties cannot be fully negotiated. A deteriorating environment coupled with falling technology costs will be the main issues focusing this, as more will become affordable both of necessity and also reduced costs. Though the environment may be an argument for one government, once the right measures are implemented it will no longer be. However the environment is certainly one hat that we can all wear. When it comes to drastic action with nuclear weapons, leaders do consider that a nuclear war would have fallout way beyond the countries involved, and a lot of responsibility in this is the dichotomy of care for the earth and care for the self for not being blamed for harming the earth. One hat, all nuclear leaders all with the power to destroy, so far all terrified of it.

Religiously one world hat is about respect despite religious differences, respecting that not only you have a right to dignity but others too.

Cultural hats are more fun. Primarily in this age of communication, global musical and contemporary events draw people together with a feeling of being one, a few things are said though nothing too meaningful (more accurately specific in detail), with the point generally being a charity aimed at relief for a suffering people somewhere, as in Live Aid for Ethiopia, Live 8 for Third World Debt. The first one was seen as successful, the second over stepping the mark. However, there is no such thing as failure (in most situations) there is only feedback and Contemporary Artists are learning how to play politicians better. U2 lost the plot at Live 8, angry that their legitimate concerns were not being taken seriously. Within nine years U2 were making statements to the UK party conferences of not only Labour in 2004[9], but also the Conservatives in 2009[10] much to the annoyance of many who felt they had ownership of him politically[11]. Like the shrewd lobbyist, U2 had given their trinkets of value to both parties now and are in a stronger position to play them off for it, at the cost of less politically mature fans (who felt they had ownership of the band through a few albums, gigs, posters and T shirts) blaming them for speaking to 'the enemy.' The anarchist prince will note that more the good start to argue with all sides of the discourse, the less the financial lobbyist will have leverage at the same game.

As a final note, it should be noticed that Earth displays all of the signs of life by classification bar reproduction and should we start to develop and inhabit other Earth like planets then Earth will display all the defining signs of life, and would then need serious consideration about being a life form in her own right. This is based on the Gaia hypothesis[12].

She can become our joint hat of the Earth Goddess sometime in the future if we do go to other planets thus proving Gaia's reproduction. However, even if we get to other planets this process of accepting the Earth Goddess would likely be slow as any religions that did get involved would need time to contextualise Gaia within their own doctrines.

Chapter 20: Population Control

This chapter aims to get the reader to realise that we must act on population control, but with compassion.

Why it is necessary for a state to help it's vulnerable

Human nature can be broken down into many different poles, but for the purposes of the vulnerable, it needs to be broken down into the desire to acquire (including keep) or give. When we have little the desire to acquire is stronger and naturally when we have abundance the desire to give is greater. This evolved through group advantage in sharing extra spoils (critically like fruit which would otherwise rot) and evolved because of random movements and growing perceptual acquaintances leading to favours being repaid. If you had something that was of no use to you, why not give it away, especially to a potential mate? Then tools came and trinkets led to hoarding. Because barter was a fairly complicated way to do business, money came into play. Here maths hit again and the fixation with numbers, or more importantly the number of digits in a number led to money itself becoming a source of lust and the natural desire to give weakened as money does not rot.

In a Platonic State an 80% top rate tax (well, 1:5 = 83.3333% but it doesn't sound as nice) would not to some be unreasonable except people with wealth can now move very quickly and find themselves in different taxation environments which compete for these people. Therefore there are two forces on our desire to give in times of plenty, one from our days as animals which is altruistic, the other based on numerical hoarding which is selfish.

Ultimately, our consciousness with money overcame our animal instincts with food whether through natural selection, societal norming or both Charity existed but could not be guaranteed to deliver all that is required all the time. However, few lived in the cities, most on the land and so money was not very high on the agenda. However, the Industrial Revolution totally reversed the situation and people more and more went to live in the towns which meant that they did not have land and so had greater need for money, but also had people closer so they could more easily form altruistic collective views on matters. Socialism started as a concept both as an ideal about altruism but also from a grim reality that too few of us would give enough to charity to bring about this altruism. The implications were that 'giving' had to be done centrally, albeit in the form of the state rather than through the tribes that had been lost in Britain years before. It is a question of whether a human being who is alive 'should' feel altruism towards others. Altruism developed in us before hoarding of money and so should be considered in the argument with at least the same weight as said monies. Insulin developed before hoarding and without insulin we would die, likely too without altruism.

Altruism expressed through the state comes in the form of helping where it is needed and desired, particularly with those in a vulnerable state, which any of us can be afflicted with at any point. Of course with an altruistic state, the whole process is systematised and will inevitably fall foul of fraud attempts. This is important: when people feel their money is being wasted the hoarding selfishness comes in and can overpower the altruism. An altruistic state that helps it's vulnerable is seen as a virtuous state, but a state that is seen to waste resources in its bid to help the vulnerable is seen as either foolish or corrupt. In these situations it gets forgotten that this does not make altruism bad, rather the state inept.

The result of this in any altruistically pointed state is that Governments of help will lead to mistakes and waste, seen as the excess of improper checks, earning contempt. This is followed by a Government of financial tightening that ultimately ends up with the corruption of the elite losing sight of the vulnerable and the elite's excesses earning contempt before the cycle repeats and an altruistic government is returned. This is both a societal negative feedback and learning system, each time a party comes into power it does try to do better than 'last time.' It is also the basis of the left right divide wherever the centre is defined in a given country.

As a brief aside, the movements of elites and other societies within society are known to lead to knowledge and network pools which have the same characteristics as a biological brain when herd moods (from hormones and images) and (neural or social) connections are taken into account. Society is one big fast, middle, and slow communicating brain, and that is why democracies are known to mature.

Why we need to keep population down
This is a trivial application of the fact that the planet is finite, and thus resources.

Why we cannot afford food aid to states if the requirement is because they have recklessly let their populations run away
This is not an argument against military, earthquake, volcano, tidal, hurricane, or drought relief. That would be both immoral and unnatural. However, for all efforts on control of consumption however it is measured, if the population doubles, no trickery can escape its effects. States which keep growing in numbers have a responsibility to ensure that they can sustain the peoples in their country. If they fail, then they need to take responsibility. This is not an argument to starve people because their states have not taken control, but to use aid as a lever to ensure that the state will take responsibility for population control if population numbers are unsustainable. If that state will not, then the aid should stop. This is not a light argument, it is not aimed at starving people but facing up to the environmental reality that if we do not control our population, many more will suffer than if we control things where they are going wrong initially.

Chapter 21: The Eternal City of the damned.

This chapter aims to show that lost souls will always pop up, and that no government can claim misery is over.

The fire of failure

Failure is actual in both the internal and existential senses. Failure in the self reduces self worth albeit for a while, existentially it gets projected back to you again for a while, but a more variable while: The greater the impact of the failure in relation to the impact of your successes, the longer the projections of both yourself and others onto you. It should also be noted that in a game of football that if you do nothing bar score a goal and then be entirely responsible for the conceding of one, you are of no use to the team and would be better out of it, successes weigh less than failures because of the space we must justify. Success works existentially in the opposite way, if you score two for the team but only concede one, your space is not just justified, but totally relished in the team with all the positive projections that come with it.

These projections can all too easily affect the internal state, it is fair to say that you should not wear your heart on your sleeve, but we are irritable beings and need to adjust to our environments and so take cues off our environment including projections. We move from one attempted accomplishment to the next and projections of failure taken in to the self cause internal conflict especially if that person has already given up on their societal context. It is this pain of giving up that is the fire of failure.

How the broken petals of love destroy

When all is going well, unless arrogance is not controlled, a natural charisma arises in the individual and their aura (which is where internal feelings and the existential projections meet), and love is easier to find in others. When all is going wrong loved ones are needed to keep the petals of love in the individual alive. If those petals break due to lack of or broken input, the fire of failure is placed on the individual. It is no surprise therefore that children without families are more likely to end up homeless, with serious addictions and (often under) selling themselves in prostitution. They have not had the feelings of self worth placed upon them, by parents, siblings, extended family and because of all of this often even stable relationships are hard to find.

Bearing this in mind, it is no surprise that men in the fire often have a lack of an extended circle of family and friends or the emotional instability of a troubled youth or both.

This breaking of petals leads to the fire of failure and can lead to chemical dependencies, debt, and ultimately homelessness or death.

Homelessness is not necessarily important to local politicians

The best way to attract the homeless to an area is to house them, feed them or even give them money. Local authorities know that if they house the homeless, word spreads and they get more homeless on their streets looking for housing. Perversely this means that the better a local authority performs, the more it gets on its books (which cost their taxpayers) if neighbouring authorities do not house their homeless. Politicians may have the most noble of intents at heart but are subject to voters' pleasure and some have deemed sentiments to the homeless as vote losers if they help, whilst others are just callous[1]. Therefore the issue does not get the consideration that it deserves, the homeless being amongst the most highly vulnerable in society.

If we are to make homelessness an issue for local politicians, they must feel that neighbouring authorities are pulling their weight too and this needs central government control, as the easiest route for innoble politicians is steer the homeless away from their area by not caring for them. In essence this is the ruination of the commons, but in reverse, instead of authorities wanting too many cattle, they want too few humans[2]. One easy way of resolving this is to get homeless to register at a government office and be asked to give a distance away from that point that they would be willing to live in still. They would then be put on a list in all relevant authorities, and the government could record results, form league tables and fine authorities that did not come up to a basic standard of housing homeless.

In saying this, it should be noted that a refugee on the streets is no more or less valuable than a home national on the streets, it is the state that they are in that should count, not the state that they are from.

The pyre of life

Unfortunately if you have a bath, you get dirty again. Unfortunately if you clear up homelessness another group of people find their lives totally disintegrating. This is the pyre of life in the eternal city of the damned, the generalised problems will never go away, but the individual problems can be resolved. People whose lives have disintegrated, need value placed upon them even if it is the proxy of society through the state and the people immediately working with them to reintegrate them into society. The archetypal images of someone at the bottom will never go, but the hand up back into society with all the detraumatisation that that gives need never go either. The fire of the pyre will never fully go, but the flames can be doused enough to help people off, even if more will inevitably fall onto it. These are the most vulnerable and it is no positive reflection on a market economy society if their needs are not addressed.

Chapter 22: On Fairness in cost in court

This chapter aims to show that justice needs to be formalised, but that formality has to allow both sides fair representation.

On how the right of defence is legal not social

In a legal trail, the defence is entitled to hear and respond to every piece of evidence that is being used to picture them as having committed an act that has been legally defined. In the court of public opinion, no matter how small or how big that court, most 'evidence' is kept from the individual and politicians use this to character assassinate with 'briefings.' Politics as a science has shown that negative briefings outweigh positive ones, again because if you are seen to have scored one goal at each end in a football game regularly you should not be in the team. These briefings can reduce a person to definitions below that of a dog, which in turn allow the accusers to deny a person all of their human rights thus proving how in the face of power they are not worth the paper that they are written on. Newspapers have to hold back from calling for people's death. The contemporary industry does not: recently Lily Allen in the song 'Fuck You' has called for someone (unnamed) to be 'slew,' Primal Scream in 'Zombie Man' questions the need for human 'sacrifice' and The Yeah Yeah Yeahs in 'Heads will roll,' allude strongly for someone else (unnamed) to be decapitated, 'Off off off with your head, dance dance dance, until you're dead.' If the preservation of all of the names of all these people were kept utterly secret, there would not be danger, but corruption in human nature cannot guarantee this.

 That is why legal constructs are needed if someone is to have a defence, because the court of public of public opinion does not have these constructs, though that is sometimes politically desired by the less virtuous.

On allocation of funds to ensure fair representation

If someone is to take another to court, it is assumed that they have the funds (or some form of legal aid) or legal prosecutors are involved because the alleged act is seen as criminal. In all cases the plaintiff has funds. McDonalds v Morris and Steel showed a case where McDonalds spent millions trying to prove libel. Morris and Steel managed to fundraise less than £100,000[1]. The imbalance between the two sides was close to 100 pounds spent on the case by McDonalds for every pound spent by the defence. This clearly has nothing to do with all being equal in front of the law. This for McDonalds turned into a means of oppressing the opinions of people or organisations significantly poorer than them.

There is a way around this. If A takes on B, in a blind auction A is asked to nominate a sum of cost budget. B is asked to do the same. A gets on fifth of B's funds, B gets one fifth of A's funds. The judge at the end of the trail has the discretion to award costs as he or she sees fit along with any potential damages, thus keeping control of people wasting the court's time. The result of this is that each side has a fighting fund of at least a quarter that of the other side, thus implementing a fairer financial playing field.

This is not just virtuous in its aim, but in a world controlled more and more by multinational companies with billions at their disposal, it is a way of stopping companies using the law as a tool of oppression.

On the brighter side, in the McLibel case, McDonalds were happy to forget about it as quickly as possible, the media had given them a hiding. If this could be guaranteed for every case it would be ideal, but too many cases are not of the scale to encourage full national media coverage, hence it is important to have level financial playing fields in court.

Chapter 23: On matters of education

This chapter aims to show that not doing (or having the power to do) a child down in the short term can all too easily destroy them in the long term.

Why there can be only one person in charge

Human psychology requires the knowledge of who has power in a situation. This stems from our troop view point from our days as chimpanzees. A teacher in a class needs to be the (alpha) arbiter of power or the children often play up, disrupt and learn significantly less. Some teachers have an innate ability to control a class with fear, respect, clarity, attentiveness, understanding and humour. Not all teachers are strong enough in all of these areas to be able to hold a group of high energy children under control.

On physical power and disruption

The right for parents to smack draws strong emotions, but without leaving marks many parents wish to protect this right. The arguments run two ways, some parents argue that a parent should be able to mentally control a child in a situation, whilst other parents argue that they simply cannot control their kids without smacking.

The same applies for teachers.

This does not mean every teacher should be able to smack, but parents have the right to give the school head the authority to 'gym shoe' if a child's behaviour is going to lead to exclusion from that school and so wreck their education totally. Other measures may be resorted to, namely formal corporal punishment can be used as well as more imaginative weekend detentions.

Children could physically grow at a far faster rate than they do, as with other mammals, but because of the learning time required to be able to deal with adulthood, their bodies do not grow until later so that whilst they are enduring terrible bouts of behaviour they can be physically controlled by an adult that is not afraid, thus not defensive, thus not overly aggressive to the child. Kinetics can be used before a gentle smack, simply give a message holding the child's arm and squeeze a bit whilst making the behavioural line to be remembered. This is use of physicality without pain.

Currently if teachers physically chastise children even on extreme provocation through physical attack, they lose their jobs. The child faces no real sanction. The child that wishes to be unruly is in control and normally totally disrupts the rest of the class. This disruption leads to less learning of and respect for the subject matter at hand for most of the remaining children in the class. The point of education is to learn, understand and respect the various tools, physical or abstract at our disposal.

The teacher needs to be in control of any disruption, ultimately to the point of gentle force. The child does not need to be in control of any disruption in class, it should be as far away from it as possible. Unfortunately disruption goes hand in hand with loss of control, and the teaching staff need to be able to control this and in the first instance, the class teacher does. Simply referring a child to a teacher who has the authority to 'gym shoe' can in itself become a threat. This is not an argument for teachers to operate without parents consent, but parents who do not want wayward children to totally destroy their education may give the teachers the authority to act on their behalves. The result would be an extra step in the disciplinary process before a child got excluded from a school altogether. This extra step would allow a great number of children another level of warning before their education was wrecked by exclusion.

How the philosophy of not allowing anyone to fail increases the failure rate

Everyone is a failure. If adults exist who have never failed at anything, they will never achieve anything for themselves because they have not the imagination to do something stupid. Saying nobody can be a failure below a certain age is insane, if you observe a toddler building a wall with bricks they fail many times. But then they succeed. Failure is feedback by which we refine our mechanisms, or give up if our aptitudes or confidences are not up to the task, maybe to return another day. Yet we are afraid of failure, to the point that year on year British 16 and 18 test grade marks have gotten higher year on year over the past 20 years yet standing in the world education tables between 2000 and 2006 has slipped from top ten to 17th in literature and 24th in maths[1]. This is because we would sooner dumb down education for all than tell individuals they have failed. However each year, no one is allowed to 'talk down' the children's 'success,' whilst in the meantime their skills go down the mire. This is corruption and political position to the point that the current generation is destroying the future generation educationally, as currently they do with the environment, the same reason standing out for both, they cannot face up to the challenge they are failing on, ratcheting up standards. The state of the education system is not the failure of the children, rather the failure of the politicians.

The inability to give feedback to youngsters, physically or even psychologically is a greater disservice than a slap on the bum and a 'you screwed up there.' We all do screw up, and we all need to be reminded sometimes not just for our own good, but for those that we are close to, love and associate with.

Chapter 24: The need to march and take ownership

This chapter aims to show the reader that you must always leave people somewhere to walk, leaving them in a corner helps no one.

Marching for its own sake

Wherever we are, we need somewhere to go. Fashions move, technology also, expert fields of knowledge through the connections and directions between human minds are constantly trying to develop themselves, and often in highly theoretical maths there is no guarantee that new theories will ever be of practical use, though a surprising amount of fields do get to be of use. There are religions that are against alcohol, but in a society where this is legal, religions do not always campaign to change the law, rather offer services to people who want help in rehabilitation. If religion is the opium of the masses, then it is certainly going to be very helpful in getting rid of other addictions. We all march whether as individuals or as groups, we all need to feel that our lives are progressing, and this can, with good faith, be highly progressive or in the case of persecution highly oppressive. Contemporary society wishes to march and often runs into the laws of politicians who through the power they have come to, end up just wanting to control rather than help us.

 Democracy is the ultimate lever in this march, if we collectively disagree with a control, we do not need to slaughter the government, just wait until the election and continue the march. Thus democracy can hold together the many hats that we have, we can disagree within a framework. We can accept an election result in the same way as if we agree to a debate we can also accept the result of that. Any national election result is the culmination of any such set of debates. We need to march, that needs to be channelled and democracy gives us the opportunity to both stick with a direction or as is sometimes necessary change it. Like a boat sailing into the wind tacking and weaving, turning both left and right, they are both needed to get the boat upwind in the journey of life.

The Anarchist Prince is a Prince that accepts democracy and only uses violence when democracy itself has been subverted by the self appointed elites, as was the case with Nelson Mandela. If a government will go back to the people, then the violence can wait until the crucifixion at the ballot box. The moment a government refuses the people this democratic voice, violence is not a right, it is a duty to society.

Ultimately this is a book about democracy, where I see it go right and where I see it go wrong. This was not intended to be encyclopaedic, rather just aiming a few points at the dart board of life.

References

Chapter 2

1. Did the Brains Trust want an NHS in 1942? BBC Archive
http://www.bbc.co.uk/archive/nhs/5149.shtml Date accessed 14/09/2010

2. BBC William Wiblerforce - Last updated 06/08/2009
http://www.bbc.co.uk/religion/religions/christianity/people/williamwilberforce_1.shtml Date accessed 14/09/2010

3. On the PM's spokesman: Alastair Campbell - Blair's virtuous thug and now a key Tory target
http://www.independent.co.uk/opinion/on-the-pms-spokesman-alastair-campbell--blairs-virtuous-thug-and-no-w-a-key-tory-target-1153761.htm Andrew Marr, The Independent Opinion, 1 April 1998, date accessed 15 July 2010

4. BBC Upload Video http://video.google.com/videoplay?docid=-1236026913411489909# Date accessed 14/09/2010

5. at-Largely: Larisa Alexandrovna published 23/01/2010
http://www.atlargely.com/atlargely/2010/01/70year-gag-on-kelly-death-evidence-dr-david-kelly.html Date accessed 14/09/2010

Chapter 3

1. BBC News: Using computers to teach children with no teachers - written 16/07/2010
http://www.bbc.co.uk/news/technology-10663353 Date accessed 14/09/2010

Chapter 5

1. Encylopedia Britanicca - Russia: The Gorbachev era: perestroika and glasnost. Martin McCauley & Dominic Lieven http://www.britannica.com/EBchecked/topic/513251/Russia/38564/The-Gorbachev-era-perestroika-and-glasnost Date accessed 14/09/2010

2. BBC News - 1989: Romania's 'first couple' executed http://news.bbc.co.uk/onthisday/hi/dates/stories/december/25/newsid_2542000/2542623.stm Date accessed 14/09/2010

3. Encyclopedia.com - Alexander Dubček . Written 2008 http://www.encyclopedia.com/topic/Alexander_Dubcek.aspx Date accessed 14/09/2010

4. Modern History Sourcebook: Vladimir Illyich Lenin: Testament, 1922: Paul Halsall Aug 1997 http://www.fordham.edu/halsall/mod/lenin-testament.html Date accessed 14/09/2010

Chapter 8

1. UK Parliament: Constitutional Crisis http://www.parliament.uk/about/living-heritage/evolutionofparliament/houseoflords/parliamentacts/overview/constitutionalcrisis/ Date accessed 14/09/2010

2. UK Parliament: The Conservatives split http://www.parliament.uk/about/living-heritage/evolutionofparliament/houseoflords/parliamentacts/overview/conservativessplit/ Date accessed 14/09/2010

3. FT.com: Fix up the House of Commons 24/05/2009 http://www.ft.com/cms/s/0/cac5fa20-4881-11de-8870-00144feabdc0,dwp_uuid=beb2c81c-43cc-11de-a9be-00144feabdc0.html Date accessed 14/09/2010

Chapter 9

1. BBC News: Google censors itself for China 25/01/2006
http://news.bbc.co.uk/1/hi/technology/4645596.stm Date accessed 14/09/2010

2. Sun Headlines: 1/11/1990 http://sunheadlines.blogspot.com/2008/11/classics-up-yours-delors.html Date accessed 14/09/2010

3. Daily Telegraph: Encore Delors! Former EC president back to revive the constitution 22/01/2006
http://www.telegraph.co.uk/news/worldnews/europe/1508499/Encore-Delors-Former-EC-president-back-to-revive-the-constitution.html Date accessed 14/09/2010

4. CREST: Centre for Research into Elections and Social Trends: Working Paper No. 75 J.Curtis 'Was it The Sun wot won it again? The influence of newspapers in the 1997 election campaign'
http://www.crest.ox.ac.uk/papers/p75.pdf Date accessed 14/09/2010

5. National Football League NFL.com News: NFL owners approve restructured plan for Steelers ownership 17/12/2008 http://www.nfl.com/news/story/09000d5d80d680cd/article/nfl-owners-approve-restructured-plan-for-steelers-ownership Date accessed 14/09/2010

Chapter 11

1. Geevor Tin Mine: How the men were paid http://www.geevor.com/index.php?object=252 Date accessed 14/09/2010

2. Leadhills Miners Library: Oldest Subscription Library in UK
http://www.visitlanarkshire.com/attractions/historic-heritage/Leadhills-Miners-Library/ Date accessed 14/09/2010

3. The Communist Manifesto: 1848 http://www.anu.edu.au/polsci/marx/classics/manifesto.html
Date accessed 14/09/2010

4. Genocide Intervention: Cambodia
http://www.genocideintervention.net/stay_informed/genocide_past_and_present Date accessed 14/09/2010

Chapter 12

1. Knowing Exploring Indonesia: Banda Islands http://www.keindonesia.com/2010/01/kepulauan-banda-banda-islands.html Date accessed 14/09/2010

2. Hanna, Willard A. p.54 (1991). Indonesian Banda: Colonialism and its Aftermath in the Nutmeg Islands. From Wikipedia so needs checking?

Ref 2 must be checked, its pulled directly from wikipedia, but I'm not even sure that I need it.....

3. Council on Foreign Relations: The Wrong Kind of Loyalty 06/1995 http://www.foreignaffairs.com/articles/50985/george-c-herring/the-wrong-kind-of-loyalty-mcnamara-s-apology-for-vietnam?page=show Date accessed 14/09/2010

4. Taliban – Definition - Opium: http://www.wordiq.com/definition/Taliban Date accessed 14/09/2010

The author notes that this page is contested, but not in relation to opium.

5. Thr New York Times - In Afghan Fields, a Challenge to Opium's Luster - 22/05/2010 http://www.nytimes.com/2010/05/23/world/asia/23poppy.html Date accessed 14/09/2010

6. Opium levels: United Nations office on Drugs and Crime – World Drug Report 2010 p.31 http://www.unodc.org/documents/wdr/WDR_2010/World_Drug_Report_2010_lo-res.pdf

7. Tehran Times: Karzai Blames Drugs Surge on Foreign Invasion 28/06/2010: http://www.tehrantimes.com/index_View.asp?code=222060 Date accessed 14/09/2010

8. BBC News: Karzai Blames Allies for Problems 20/01/2009: http://news.bbc.co.uk/1/hi/world/south_asia/7839953.stm Date accessed 14/09/2010

9. Reuters: 28 March 2010 Diana Abdallah - Russia says U.S. should eradicate Afghan opium
http://www.reuters.com/article/idUSTRE62R0QH20100328 Date accessed 14/09/2010

Chapter 13

1. US Army Center of Military History - The United States Army in Somalia 1992-1994: last updated
24/02/2006 http://www.history.army.mil/brochures/somalia/somalia.htm Date accessed
15/09/2010

2. The Free Library: Fiasco In Pristina - 1999 MGN Ltd
http://www.thefreelibrary.com/FIASCO+IN+PRISTINA+%3A+RUSSIAN+TROOPS+ENTER+KOSOVO%3B
+Nato+left+standing...-a060451294 Date accessed 15/09/2010

3. The History Guy: The No Fly Zone War (1991-2003) http://www.historyguy.com/no-
fly_zone_war.html Date accessed 15/09/2010

4. A world transformed: President George Bush, Brent Scowcroft ISBN: 0679432485

5. Human Rights Watch - The 1991 Uprising in Iraq And Its Aftermath: June 1992
http://www.hrw.org/reports/1992/Iraq926.htm Date accessed 15/09/2010

6. BBC News: Timeline- Iraqi Kurds: 01/09/2009
http://news.bbc.co.uk/1/hi/world/middle_east/country_profiles/2893067.stm Date accessed
15/09/2010

7. BBC News: Viewpoint-Islam and London Bombings - 19/07/2005
http://news.bbc.co.uk/1/hi/uk/4693845.stm Date accessed 15/09/2010

Chapter 14

1. Times Online: The Sunday Times: Revealed: Labour lords change laws for cash - 25/01/2009
http://www.timesonline.co.uk/tol/news/politics/article5581547.ece Date accessed 15/09/2010

2. The Independent: MPs face 'cash for questions' inquiry 11/07/1994
http://www.independent.co.uk/news/mps-face-cash-for-questions-inquiry-1413008.html Date
accessed 15/09/2010

3. Times Online: The Sunday Times: Expenses scandal: House of frauds 17/05/2009
http://www.independent.co.uk/news/mps-face-cash-for-questions-inquiry-1413008.html Date
accessed 15/09/2010

4. Thomas More: Utopia - Penguin Classics 1965 translated by Paul Turner ISBN 0-14-044165-4: Book
Two p.143 footnote 30

5. Peter Ackroyd: The Life of Thomas More – Vintage ISBN 9780749386405 p.392

Chapter 15

1. European Commission: Single Market for Goods – Enterprise and Industry
http://ec.europa.eu/enterprise/policies/single-market-goods/regulatory-policies-common-rules-for-
products/new-legislative-framework/ Date accessed 15/09/2010

2. US v Microsoft: Court's findings of fact 05/11/1999
http://www.justice.gov/atr/cases/f3800/msjudgex.htm Date accessed 15/09/2010

3. BBC – History – British History In Depth: The Jarrow Crusade 05/11/2009
http://www.bbc.co.uk/history/british/britain_wwone/jarrow_01.shtml Date accessed 15/09/2010

4. New Economics Foundation: Clone Town Britain: 06/06/2005
http://www.neweconomics.org/publications/clone-town-britain Date accesssed 15/09/2010

5. BBC News: Anti-terrorist hotline ad banned for being 'offensive' 11/08/2010
http://www.bbc.co.uk/news/uk-10929203 Date accessed 15/09/2010

Chapter 16

1. BBC Upload Video: Dr David Kelly Conspiracy http://video.google.com/videoplay?docid=-1236026913411489909# Date accessed 15/09/2010

2. Essential Margaret Thatcher – The Thatcher Foundation
http://www.margaretthatcher.org/essential/biography.asp Date accessed 15/09/2010

3. BBC News: UK Politics: Heseltine – Political CV 27/04/2000
http://news.bbc.co.uk/1/hi/uk_politics/727824.stm Date accessed 15/09/2010

4. BBC News: Football - Hoddle Sacked 03/02/1999
http://news.bbc.co.uk/1/hi/sport/football/270194.stm Date accessed 15/09/2010

5. BBC World Politics: The deep roots of French Secularism 01/09/2004
http://news.bbc.co.uk/1/hi/world/europe/3325285.stm Date accessed 15/09/2010

6. BBC – Historical Figures – Vladimir Lenin (1870 – 1924)
http://www.bbc.co.uk/history/historic_figures/lenin_vladimir.shtml Date accessed 15/09/2010

7. Terje B. Englund – Velvet Revolution - Czech Expatriot Site: 26/01/2006
http://www.expats.cz/prague/article/books-literature/velvet-revolution/ Date accessed 15/09/2010

8. Central Europe Review – Sean Hanley – The Revolution That Never Was? 26/10/1998
http://www.ce-review.org/authorarchives/hanley_archive/hanley5old.html Date accessed 15/09/2010

Chapter 17

1. The Middle Ages Website - Alchin, L.K. - Queen Matilda http://www.middle-ages.org.uk/queen-matilda.htm Date accessed 15/09/2010

2. The Middle Ages Website - Alchin, L.K. – Magna Carta 1215 http://www.middle-ages.org.uk/magna-carta.htm Date accessed 15/09/2010

3. UK Parliament – End of the Protectorate http://www.parliament.uk/about/living-heritage/evolutionofparliament/parliamentaryauthority/civilwar/overview/end-of-the-protectorate/ Date accessed 15/09/2010

4. History Learning Site: Chris Truman: The 1688 Revolution http://www.historylearningsite.co.uk/1688_revolution.htm Date accessed 15/09/2010

5. UK Parliament – The Reform Act 1832 http://www.parliament.uk/about/living-heritage/evolutionofparliament/houseofcommons/reformacts/overview/reformact1832/ Date accessed 15/09/2010

6. UK Parliament – The Second Reform Act 1867 http://www.parliament.uk/about/living-heritage/evolutionofparliament/houseofcommons/reformacts/overview/furtherreformacts/ Date accessed 15/09/2010

7. UK Parliament – Third Reform Act 1884 http://www.parliament.uk/about/living-heritage/evolutionofparliament/houseofcommons/reformacts/overview/one-man-one-vote/ Date accessed 15/09/2010

8. UK Parliament - Women Get The Vote http://www.parliament.uk/about/living-heritage/transformingsociety/electionsvoting/womenvote/overview/thevote/ Date accessed 15/09/2010

9. The Guardian: New evidence of widespread fraud in Afghanistan election uncovered - 19/09/2009 http://www.guardian.co.uk/world/2009/sep/18/afghanistan-election-fraud-evidence Date accessed 15/09/2010

10. American Politics Journal: Iranian Election Fraud 2009: Who was the real target... and why? 15/06/2009 http://www.apj.us/index.php?option=com_content&task=view&id=2455&Itemid=2 Date accessed 15/09/2010

11. Centre For Research on Globalisation: Michael Keefer - Election Fraud In America 30/11/2004 http://www.globalresearch.ca/articles/KEE411D.html Date accessed 15/09/2010

12. Scotsman.com News: 'Mad, Bad Gordon Brown' ... By Tony Blair 15/07/2010 http://news.scotsman.com/politics/39Mad-bad-Gordon-Brown39-.6420587.jp Date accessed 15/09/2010

13. Falkland Islands Information Portal: The Rights and Wrongs of the Historic Claims to the Falkland Islands: http://www.falklands.info/history/hist82article11.html Date accessed 15/09/2010

14. History World: History of Argentina http://www.historyworld.net/wrldhis/PlainTextHistories.asp?ParagraphID=ntw Date accessed 15/09/2010

15. Spartacus Educational: Margaret Thatcher Biography http://www.spartacus.schoolnet.co.uk/COLDthatcher.htm Date accessed 15/09/2010

16. Encyclopedia.com Leopoldo Fortunato Galtieri Facts, information, pictures http://www.encyclopedia.com/topic/Leopoldo_Fortunato_Galtieri.aspx Date accessed 15/09/2010

Chapter 18

1. New Statesman: The rule of the chimpanzees: A.C.Grayling 23/10/2001 http://www.newstatesman.com/200104230016 Date accessed 15/09/2010

2. Biography Online: Benjamin Disraeli Biography http://www.biographyonline.net/politicians/uk/benjamin-disraeli.html Date accessed 15/09/2010

3. International Socialism Journal 85: pub 1999 New Labour, New Moralism the welfare politics and ideology of New Labour under Blair http://pubs.socialistreviewindex.org.uk/isj85/lavalette.htm Date accessed 15/09/2010

4. M.M.Ketchel 'Fertility Control Agents as a possible solution to the World Population Problem' 'Perspectives in Biology and Medication II' 1968

Chapter 19

1. BBC: History – Wars – The Soviet Union's Last Stand 05/11/2009 http://www.bbc.co.uk/history/worldwars/coldwar/soviet_stand_01.shtml Date accessed 15/09/2010

2. European People's Party: The Berlin Declaration p. 9 www.eppgroup.eu/Activities/docs/berlin_declaration/en.pdf Date accessed 15/09/2010

3. Europa: Treaty Establishing The European Economic Community 10/07/2007 http://europa.eu/legislation_summaries/institutional_affairs/treaties/treaties_eec_en.htm Date accessed 15/09/2010

4. Europa: Treaty of Maastricht on European Union 10/07/2007 http://europa.eu/legislation_summaries/economic_and_monetary_affairs/institutional_and_econo mic_framework/treaties_maastricht_en.htm Date accessed 15/09/2010

5. UK Parliament: The Resignation of The European Commission http://www.parliament.uk/commons/lib/research/rp99/rp99-032.pdf Date accessed 15/09/2010

6. Catholic Online: St Augustine of Canterbury - Terry Matz http://www.catholic.org/saints/saint.php?saint_id=25 Date accessed 15/09/2010

7. Christian Times Online A Change in Leadership Can Be Challenging - Mark Nickens http://www.christiantimelines.com/2%20then%203%20Popes.htm Date accessed 15/09/2010

8. New Advent, Heresy Kevin Knight 2009 http://www.newadvent.org/cathen/07256b.htm Date accessed 15/09/2010

9. BBC Politics: Get real on Africa urges Bono 29/09/2004 http://news.bbc.co.uk/1/hi/uk_politics/3699234.stm Date accessed 15/09/2010

10. Guardian: Bono makes surprise appearance at Tory conference 08/10/2009 http://www.guardian.co.uk/politics/2009/oct/08/bono-conservative-conference Date accessed 15/09/2010

11. Guardian: Bono becomes Twitter villain after appearing at Tory Conference 08/10/2009 http://www.guardian.co.uk/politics/2009/oct/08/bono-twitter-tory-conference Date accessed 15/09/2010

12. Gaia Theory: Gaia Theory Hypothesis 2009 http://www.gaiatheory.co.uk/category/gaia-theory/ Date accessed 15/09/2010

Chapter 21

1. Local Government Lawyer: Ombudsman criticises Hammersmith and Fulham over homeless pregnant woman case 19/01/2010 http://localgovernmentlawyer.co.uk/index.php?option=com_content&view=article&id=891%3Aombudsman-criticises-hammersmith-a-fulham-over-homeless-pregnant-woman-case&catid=52%3Aadult-social-services-articles&q=&Itemid=8 Date accessed 15/09/2010

2. Library of Economics and Liberty: Tragedy of the Commons - Garrett Harding 2008 http://www.econlib.org/library/Enc/TragedyoftheCommons.html Date accessed 15/09/2010

Chapter 22

1. BBC News: McLibel the longest case in English History 15/03/2005 http://news.bbc.co.uk/1/hi/uk/4266741.stm Date accessed 15/09/2010

Chapter 23

1. BBC News: Education: UK schools slip down global table 04/12/2007
http://news.bbc.co.uk/1/hi/7115692.stm Date accessed 15/09/2010

Printed in Great Britain
by Amazon.co.uk, Ltd.,
Marston Gate.

Looking at
Local Records

_____ Joy Richardson _____

Batsford Academic and Educational Ltd   London

Typeset by Tek-Art Ltd, London SE20
and printed in Great Britain by
R.J. Acford
Chichester, Sussex
for the publishers
Batsford Academic and Educational Ltd,
an imprint of B. T. Batsford Ltd,
4 Fitzhardinge Street,
London W1H 0AH

ISBN 0 7134 3664 6

Frontispiece   A German caricature, from a series
called "The Bad Pen".

_____ ACKNOWLEDGMENT _____

The Author and Publishers would like to
thank the following for their permission to
use illustrations in the book: The Diocesan
Registry, Little Comberton, Pershore, fig 12;
East Sussex Record Office, figs 6 and 16
(The Reverend F.R. Cumberlege, Rector of
St Clement with All Saints, Hastings), 17
(Canon D. Maundrell, Team Rector of Rye),
18 (The Reverend J.G.P. Habgood, Team
Rector of Lewes), 43, 45; Essex Record
Office, figs 4, 10 (Q/RDc 15), 19 (Q/SBb
334/15), 20 (Q/SBb 334/72, 21 (Q/SBa
2/115), 24 (Q/SBb 249/16), 26, 27 (Q/
RDc 15), 28 (Q/RDc 15), 29 (D/CT 54), 30
(D/DHt p15), 31 (D/CT54 (sheet 5)), 32
(XLIII 12); Glamorgan Archive Service, fig
44; Glinton Primary School, Glinton, Cambs,
figs 11 and 37, 36; Leicestershire Record
Office, fig 25 (QS 79/1/1); Lincolnshire
Archives Office, figs 5 (Misc. Dep. 264/1), 7
and 14 (Cowbit par. 12), 23 (Cowbit par.
13), 33 (probate inventory 192/328), 39
(Huttoft par. 16/4), 42 (1851 Census Report,
Vol 11, Div IX, p.28); Mansell Collection,
the frontispiece and figs 2, 3; Newborough
Primary School, Newborough, Cambs, fig
38; Northamptonshire Record Office, figs 1,
8 and 13 (136P/133/2), 9 and 35, 15 (136P/
60), 22 (261P/220/3), 34, 46, 47 (ZA 8743);
Public Record Office, London, fig 41 (HO
107/2177).

Contents

The
Illustrations

1
Introduction

The people died long ago. Their possessions have been dispersed or destroyed and their houses pulled down or modernized. Yet the written records of their personal and official affairs have survived in large quantities. These local records tell us who lived when and where, what work they did and what their houses were like. They show how communities were organized and how justice was administered. They speak in the official language of the law, and also in the words of ordinary people.

From these records, patterns of existence which have long since disappeared can be pieced together again, and our understanding of the here and now can be made richer by greater familiarity with what went before.

This book provides an introduction to a wide range of local records, which are readily available throughout England and Wales. Each section looks at a group of records, explaining their original purpose, the information they provide, and where they can be found today. Documents are reproduced in each section to give a typical example of each type of record, and to show how it was set out. These examples have been collected together from many different parts of the country.

Local records now have a better chance of survival than ever before. In the past, such records were widely dispersed. County Councils held old County Records, many

Church Records were in Diocesan Record Offices, and parishes still kept most of their records in old parish chests. In the last fifty years, Record Offices (sometimes called "Archives Offices") have been set up in every county. They have become the collecting-point for local records of every kind. In addition, some large cities have their own Record Offices, dealing specifically with Borough Records, and many large libraries have good local history sections.

Local records fall into a number of broad categories (each containing many different types of records):

— County Records from the Quarter Sessions and later from County Councils.
— Borough Records concerning the independent activities of towns.
— Parish Records of church affairs, and secular administration.
— Diocesan Records, relating to the church's wider responsibilities.
— Estate and Family Records, collected and deposited by individuals.

The records in Record Offices are usually organized in these main categories, and there may also be catalogues for specific types of records, such as maps, enclosure awards and inventories. Alphabetical indexes are usually available to help you track down records concerning a particular PERSON, PLACE or

▲

SUBJECT. Once you have found a record in an index or catalogue, it can be ordered by its reference number from the store-room where it is usually kept.

Most Record Offices are open each weekday, and can be visited by appointment. Archivists are available to give help and advice, but they have many other jobs to do, so it is helpful if you can come with a clear idea of what you are looking for. Some Record Offices have an Education Officer who is able to visit schools, and provide advice about local records, as well as giving help in the Record Office itself. In many cases it will be necessary for teachers to search out the documents which are appropriate for use in school, though local history groups may have covered the ground already and be able to give advice. Record Offices

1 The index room of the Northamptonshire Record Office, which houses the finding aids such as catalogues, summary lists and indexes, along with microfilm readers.

generally provide a good photocopying service, and photocopies or photostats can be made of most documents.

The availability of local records, in original, photocopied or even printed form, makes it possible for us to "listen in" across the centuries to the words of the original writers. Historical awareness takes on a new dimension as we follow the threads of change and development through the lives of particular communities, learning to recognize the pattern of the ordinary, and being constantly surprised by the discovery of the extraordinary.

2
The Making
of Local Records

Materials

In a world which changed slowly, written records, like the institutions they reflected, were expected to endure. The survival of many documents can be attributed to the use of parchment, which is far more robust than paper. Parchment was used for all official documents during the Middle Ages, and it continued to be used extensively into the nineteenth century.

Parchment is made from animal skins (usually sheep or goat), which were soaked, scraped and stretched to remove the hair and reduce the thickness of the skin. They were then dried on frames, and the surface was smoothed and treated ready for use. The parchment could then be used as individual sheets, made into a book, or bound with cords into a roll. The flesh side is smoother and whiter than the hair side, and was always used in preference when only one side was needed. Vellum is a high-quality parchment made from the skins of young animals, particularly calves.

Paper came into use in England during the fourteenth century, and was found useful for mundane purposes such as writing letters and keeping household accounts. The use of paper gradually increased, but England did not make its own paper until the end of the seventeenth century, and many of the types of records discussed in this book may be found on either parchment or paper.

The growth of printing led to a greater use of paper, but the creation of the "one-off" document remained unmechanized until the invention of the typewriter. As a result, the use of pen and ink on parchment continued into Victorian times, as can be seen in many enclosure awards.

Until the development of the steel pen around 1830, the most popular writing tool was the goose or swan quill. The quill was cut at an oblique angle, which gave a clear contrast between thin and thick strokes. The softness of the quill meant that it needed frequent re-cutting (hence the importance of the "pen-knife"). The steel pen, which led to the development of Victorian copperplate handwriting, had a pointed end and kept its sharpness. Contrast could only be achieved by pressing hard on the down-strokes, to release more ink.

Recipes for ink, dating from the Middle Ages, give oak-apples (galls), vitriol and gum as the principal ingredients, diluted with water. The secret lay in the combination of iron from the vitriol and acid from the galls. This produced a very durable, black ink which bit into the paper and could not be removed. Carbon came into use later, to increase the blackness of ink, but carbon-based inks lack the permanence of iron inks. For use with steel nibs, ink had to be very

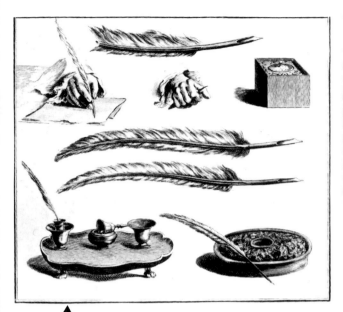

▲
2 Eighteenth-century quills, pen-knife, ink-wells and sandbox. Sand was used to dry the ink.

liquid so that it would flow easily, but it was also likely to fade more quickly.

Language

During the Middle Ages most official documents were written in Latin. English, however, was used more and more as administration and business activity grew under the Tudors, creating an increased demand for written documents of all kinds. Latin was banned altogether under Oliver Cromwell, but the Restoration of Charles II brought a temporary return to more traditional ways. Latin remained the official language of law and the law courts until it was finally discarded by an Act of Parliament in 1733, though by then it was often used only for

The course of a true love letter runs smoothest when written with one of C BRANDAUER & CO S Circular pointed Pens These pens neither scratch nor spurt the points being rounded by a new process. C B & Co also manufacture J Pens, School Pens, turned up points, turned down points, curved, square, and slanting nibbled, and every other description of Steel Pens Six Prize Medals awarded Assorted Sample Box, 6d of any Stationer, or post free 7 stamps, from C BRANDAUER & CO S Pen Works Birmingham ; or from their Wholesale Warehouse, 24, King Edward Street, London E C

▲
3   An advertisement of 1886.

the formal beginnings and endings of documents.

The documents reproduced in this book date from the seventeenth century onwards, and Latin appears only in words and phrases which had become part of the English language.

8

3
Reading
the Documents

The study of the writing on old documents is known as "palaeography". Interpreting an ancient document in an unfamiliar handwriting can appear a daunting task, but, at the simplest level, it can be tackled rather like the piecing together of a jigsaw or the solving of a crossword puzzle. The documents reproduced in this book are intended for you to practise on, and you can check your efforts against the transcripts included at the end of the book on pages 60-66.

Beware of trying to get to the overall meaning too quickly. Allow yourself time to read letter-by-letter and word-by-word, in order to carry out the detective work involved in cracking the handwriting code. A few lines are usually enough to provide examples of all the main letter forms used by a writer, so it may help to mask off the rest of the

4   The Secretarie Alphabete from *A Book Containing Divers Sortes of Hands*, 1571.
▼

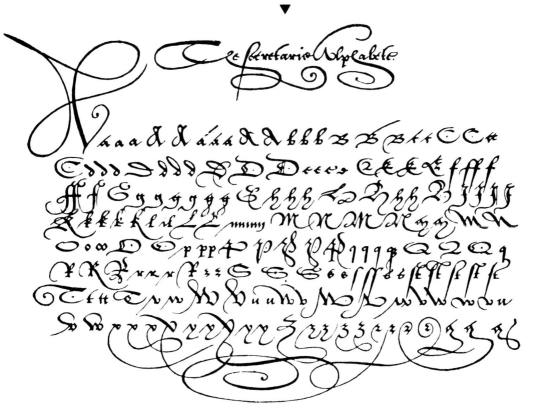

5 Petition for Enclosure, 1629
This is written in typical Secretary Hand. The style is upright, but the top of the letter "d" slopes backwards. Try to recognize the letter shapes used for e, c, s, r and h, as these are the most likely to cause confusion. No distinction is made between i and j.

e	ℰ ℯ ∂	r	u ʒ
c	r	h	ℎ ℰ
s	∫ ß	y	y

◄ 6 Parish Register, 1676
This shows a formal or "engrossing" style of Secretary Hand. Note the diamond-shaped letters which are frequently unjoined, and the strong contrast between thick and thin strokes. A run of "minims" or parallel down-strokes in letters such as i, n, m and u can make them difficult to distinguish. Notice the two different shapes used for s.

7 Instruction to make Hue and Cry, 1697
Secretary Hand was increasingly modified by italic, which originated in Italy at the time of the Renaissance. The italic influence is seen in this extract, which shows a forward-sloping writing and rounded letter shapes which could be easily joined in a rapid flowing style.

r	ʒ	y	y
s	ß ∫ s	H	ℎ
e	ℯ	th	ℎ
p	p	and	ℰ

document and to work on a small section at a time. Familiarity with handwriting styles grows quickly if you can build up your own inventory of the letter shapes used in a particular document, and then carry this on from one document to the next. The context may tell you what a word could be, but never accept a solution as final until you have checked it out letter-by-letter, or you may be led off on entirely the wrong track.

The Development of Handwriting Styles

The major documents of government in the Middle Ages were highly formal and were

8 Churchwarden's Accounts, 1710
From 1700 onwards there was a rapid development in the use of round hand, with its strong forward slope and the gradual addition of loops to ascenders and descenders. This extract shows the influence of round hand, as well as the use of traditional letter forms for c, e and r.

9 Codicil to John Clifton's Will, 1783
This shows a fully developed round hand, the basic form of which has continued into the present. There are personal flourishes, such as the down turn at the end of words, but the letter shapes have reached their modern forms and are easily recognizable.

▼

drawn up by professional scribes in a laborious and stylized hand. As the administrative concerns of church and state expanded, at both central and local parish levels, the need grew for a quick and easy handwriting style for the ordinary man which could also be used for formal and official purposes. This led to the development of "Secretary Hand" which, in a variety of forms, was the basic handwriting used in English documents between 1550 and 1700. The characteristic letter shapes of Secretary Hand are illustrated in figure 4.

Secretary Hand was gradually modified by italic, and later gave way to the development of modern round hand. The extracts in figures 5 to 11 (from documents which are reproduced more fully elsewhere in the book) show how handwriting developed from the seventeenth to the nineteenth centuries, and provide an introduction to characteristic letter forms.

There are some general points which need bearing in mind when reading old handwritten documents.

10 Enclosure Award, 1818
Engrossing hand continued to be used throughout the nineteenth century for formal documents, including Acts of Parliament, enclosure agreements and title deeds. It was written with a quill which bit into the writing surface, making clear contrasts between the thick and thin strokes of the pen.

▼

The children are in good order: the Girls'
Needlework deserves praise, and the singing
by note was fairly good — otherwise the results
of the examination are far from satisfactory,
especially in Spelling; not a single child
passed in Writing in the third Standard.

▲
11 *School Inspector's Report 1886*
This shows the development of Victorian cursive handwriting, with its elongated ascenders and descenders, and the characteristically fine lines and lack of contrast which mark the change from quill to steel pen.

Capital Letters

Capital letters were used frequently and randomly and have no particular significance. It is often difficult to distinguish between small and capital letters when they share the same basic form, as was frequently the case in eighteenth-century round hand. I and J may well be identical (as in the codicil to John Clifton's will, figure 9). There was no capital F until the eighteenth century, so ff was used instead.

Punctuation

The consistent use of full stops to mark the end of sentences is a fairly modern development and occurs rarely in the documents included in this book. As a result, it is often difficult to unravel the structure of individual sentences, which are strung together by the use of "and" or in later documents may be broken up by commas. Capital letters may mark the beginning of a new sentence, but they were so widely used that they give little guidance. Curly lines were often used to fill empty gaps at the ends of lines and were purely decorative.

Spelling

Spelling in pre-dictionary days tended to be personal and erratic, becoming more consistent during the eighteenth century. Some words were even spelt several different ways by the same writer within one document. Vowels were frequently interchanged. Many variations were used for combinations such as "ea" or "ou", and "ie"/"ei" caused even more confusion than they do today (as in "feild" and "forfiet"). "e" was often added to the ends of words (as in "keepe", or "rome" for room). "c", "k" and "ck" were interchangeable; so too were "c" and "t", particularly in words ending with "tion" (as in "peticon" and "consideracon"). Double and single consonants were used fairly randomly (as in "comand" and "perill").

Abbreviations

The formal use of Latin in legal documents resulted in widespread abbreviation. This declined with the use of English and the development of speedier handwriting, but several forms of abbreviation are worth noting:

— the colon, as in ch: (church), Geo: (George), Maj: ^{ties} (Majesties).
— the raised ending, as in y^e (the), y^t (that), wth (with), W^m(William).
— the straight line, or curly flourish over a word, ab̄t (about), s̄d (said), Anno Dom̃ (Anno Domini).
— y, as in the familiar "ye" (the) is the old Anglo-Saxon form for "th".
— most frequently used of all is the sign for "and", known as the ampersand.

4
Parish Records

England was already divided into parishes before the Norman Conquest, each with its own church and its own priest. During the Middle Ages, parishioners became accustomed to keeping the church in good repair, and raising the money to do this. Parish meetings (known as "vestries", because they were held in the church vestry) were called, and Churchwardens were appointed to oversee church affairs.

The Tudors found this ready-made system very useful, and heaped extra duties and responsibilities onto the parish. As well as being responsible for the spiritual welfare of its inhabitants, the parish was now required to provide arms for soldiers, care for the wounded, repair for the roads, and relief for the poor.

All this needed money and people to carry out the work involved. Vestry meetings were held at least once a year. Some vestries were controlled by a small and select body of citizens, but many others were open to the whole parish. At these meetings, officers were elected by their fellow-parishioners, to serve for the coming year, and Church Rates were fixed, to cover expenditure. Service as Churchwarden, Highways Surveyor, Overseer of the Poor or Constable may often have seemed a chore, but it meant that many ordinary people took an active part in local government in a way which is rarely possible today.

There were few laws to dictate how parish affairs should be organized and every parish operated slightly differently. The Quarter Sessions were able to deal with serious matters, but usually, if the roads were full of potholes or the peace was being disturbed by unruly behaviour, it was left to the parish to sort things out for itself.

In Tudor times all parishes were instructed to provide chests to keep parish registers in. They also had to provide a strong chest with a hole in the top, for the collection of alms for the poor. It was to have three keys, of which the Vicar and Churchwardens were each to hold one. One chest usually served both purposes and, over the centuries, registers, account books and a whole variety of other documents accumulated in it. This list gives an idea of what one such chest used to hold before its contents were transferred to the local Record Office for safe-keeping:

Registers of Baptisms, Marriages and Burials
Papers about parish charities
Churchwardens' bills and accounts
Minutes from Vestry meetings
Overseers of the Poor account books
Documents concerning responsibility for vagrants and bastards
Apprenticeship indentures for pauper children
Surveyors of the Highways' accounts
Notices about Enclosures

12 Glebe Terrier of property and land belonging to the Vicarage of Broadway, Worcestershire, 1715. (Transcript on page 60)

The chest itself was often a magnificent piece of furniture, and many still survive in parish churches today.

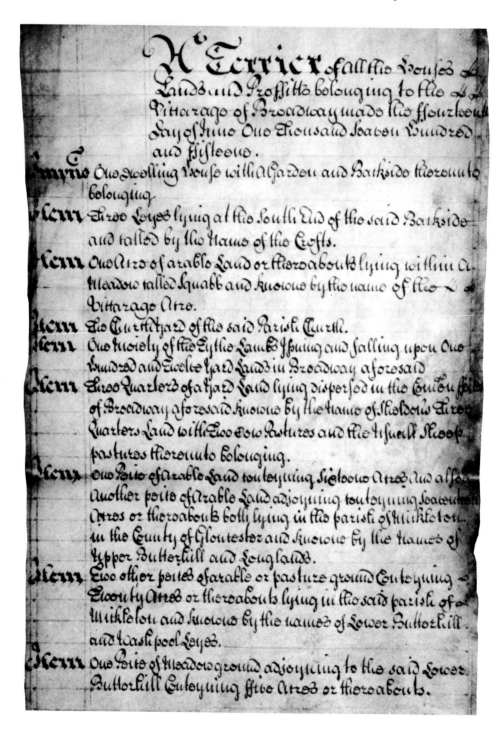

Glebe Terriers

In many parishes, the church owned a lot of land. This was known as "glebe" land, and was a great help to the church's finances. Some of it was farmed by the Vicar himself, but much of it was rented out. The Bishops in each diocese liked to keep up-to-date information on the church's possessions. Each parish was visited regularly and, in preparation for these visitations, the Vicar, Churchwardens and main landowners drew up a "Glebe Terrier". This gave detailed information about the vicarage, the church and churchyard, and the glebe lands.

Terriers vary widely in the amount of information they provide, but the size and layout of the vicarage is often described, giving a clear impression of the Vicar's style of life. Most terriers give a full description of church lands held in various parts of the parish.

Large numbers of terriers have survived from the seventeenth, eighteenth and nineteenth centuries and they provide valuable details about field names, the state of en-

13   Churchwarden's Accounts for Glinton in Cambridgeshire (formerly Northamptonshire), 1710. (Transcript on page 66)

closure and types of agriculture. The glebe terrier in figure 12 gives a lot of information about the names of fields in the parish and what they were being used for at the time.

Churchwardens' Accounts

There were usually two Churchwardens, and if the Vicar and vestry could not agree on their choice, they appointed one each. The Churchwardens were responsible for the church and its upkeep. They had to provide the bread and wine for communion, make sure the church was properly furnished, undertake repairs to the building and ensure that the parishioners attended church regularly. The church was the social centre of the parish and the wardens distributed ale and arranged feasts at times of rejoicing. They also had secular responsibilities, such as keeping down vermin and seeing that buckets, thatch-hooks and other fire-fighting equipment was available at the church. At many points, their duties overlapped with those of other officers, particularly in looking after the needs of the poor.

The page from a Churchwarden's Account Book for 1710 shown in figure 13 records just this range of responsibilities. The church gate and porch needed repair, and stone, lime, sand and gravel were required for this. Transport from the quarry had to be arranged and tolls paid along the way. The flagon for communion wine and the church door key also needed mending. The clock needed attention and the Vicar's surplice had to be washed and mended. In an effort to keep "vermin" down, money was paid for the capture of a badger and a hedgehog. The country was at war at the time, and English victories over the French were marked by bell-ringing and ale-drinking . . . all organized by the Churchwarden!

Constables

The office of Constable originated in the Middle Ages. Constables were originally appointed by manor courts, to maintain law and order in towns. In time, Parish or "Petty" Constables in effect became parish officers elected by the parish vestry, though their appointment had to be confirmed by the Justices of the Peace before whom they were summoned to take an oath of loyalty.

Most parishes had two Constables, elected for a year at a time. The responsibilities of a Constable were many and varied. He had to supervise the training of the local militia and the supply of arms. Criminals had to be arrested and beggars moved on. There were ale-houses to be inspected, and the punishment of wrongdoers in the local stocks to be seen to. It even fell to the Constable's lot to look after the parish bull! He also had to assist other parish officers in convening parish meetings, enforcing regular attendance at church and seeing to the welfare of the poor. On top of that, he had to carry out the instructions of the Quarter Sessions, collect the money for the County Rate, and act as agent for the raising of special national taxes. Small wonder that the job of Constable was an unpopular one, to be avoided if at all possible!

The instruction to make Hue and Cry (figure 14) shows how much the enforcement of law and order depended on the vigilance of the amateur, unpaid and often reluctant Constable. If either of the men named was sighted, the Constable was to raise the alarm and call out other law-abiding citizens in pursuit. Many other aspects of the Constable's job are revealed in accounts which were kept. Parish Constables were finally relieved of their responsibilities when the County Police Act of 1839 led to the setting up of paid police forces within each county.

Highways Surveyors

The appalling state of the roads led to the passing of the Highways Act in 1555. This laid down a system for maintaining the roads

▲

14　Instructions to make Hue and Cry, sent to the Constables in Cowbit, Lincolnshire, 1697. (Transcript on page 65)

which remained in force for almost 300 years. Parishioners had to work (or provide someone else to work) on the roads for a set number of days each year and had to provide carts for the carrying of stone and gravel. Surveyors were elected annually to make sure that the work was done and that the roads were kept in good repair. The office was unpaid and highly unpopular, as it was time-consuming and involved forcing your neighbours into work they disliked. Like the Constables, the Highways Surveyors were responsible to the Court of Quarter Sessions, who dealt with complaints but generally left the Surveyors to get on with the job as best they could. This pattern continued until the General Highways Act of 1835, which set up Highway Boards to look after the roads, thus relieving the parish of another of its ancient responsibilities.

The extract from a Highways Surveyor's Account Book (figure 15) shows some of the work involved in organizing teams to work, collecting gravel and other materials, and providing ale to keep the men going!

Where to Find Parish Records

The records for most parishes have now been deposited in Record Offices, where they are catalogued under the name of the parish. Where records have remained in the parish, they may still be in the parish chest, and can be seen with the Vicar's permission.

Churchwarden's Accounts will be listed in the parish records. Highways Surveyors' and Constables' Accounts may also be listed, but other papers concerning their activities may be found in the Quarter Sessions Records in the Record Office.

Glebe Terriers went to the Diocesan Registry. They are classed as Diocesan

Records, but most dioceses have now deposited these records in County Record Offices. Some terriers were left in the parish chest and are listed with parish records.

Questions Parish Records Can Help to Answer

What was the Vicarage like and how much land was owned by the church? (Glebe Terriers)

How was law and order maintained in the parish? (Constables' papers)

What was involved in keeping up the roads? (Highways Surveyors' Accounts)

How did the parishioners organize their own affairs? (Vestry Minutes)

How were the poor looked after? (Charity papers, Overseers' Accounts and documents relating to the relief of the poor — see pages 27-31)

How important was the church in the life of the parish? (Churchwardens' Accounts)

15   Highways Surveyor's Accounts for Glinton in Cambridgeshire (formerly Northamptonshire), 1793. (Transcript on page 61)

▼

The Disbursments of John Higginton Surveyor of the Highways from Mich. 1792, to D° 1793.

5
Parish Registers

Parish Registers are the most widely available of all parish records. In 1538, Thomas Cromwell (Henry VIII's secretary) ordered the Vicar or Rector of each parish to record in a book every christening, marriage and burial which took place in his church, and to keep these registers locked up in a "sure coffer". These early registers were often written on loose sheets of paper, and in 1598 clergy were instructed to copy them up properly into parchment books. Some parishes have registers surviving from the

16   Parish Register for All Saints, Hastings, Sussex, 1676. (Transcript on page 64)

▼

Banns of Marriage _Between Thomas Brown Sojourner in this Parish, Ann Kennard_
Published on the 24th & 31st Days of October & on the 7th day of Nov.r 1756 by George Carleton Vicar

N.º _80._ The said _Thomas Brown_ of ~~the~~ Parish _of Rye in the County of_
Sussex Carpenter and _Ann Kennard_ of _the_
Parish _of Rye in the County of Sussex Spinster_ were
Married in this _Church_ by _Banns by Consent of their Parents_
this _Tenth_ Day of _November_ in the Year One Thousand Seven
Hundred and _Fifty Six_ by me _Geo: Carleton Vicar of Rye_
This Marriage was solemnized between Us { _Thomas Brownzier_
Ann ╞ Kennard
mark
In the Presence of _Will.m Croucher_
John Dadd

▲
17   Marriage Register for Rye, Sussex, 1756.

sixteenth century, but many more date from the seventeenth century onwards.

In these early registers, the records were kept in a variety of ways. Baptisms, marriages and burials were sometimes recorded in separate columns (see figure 16), but more often they were mixed together in a simple chronological list. The amount of information given also varies widely. From 1666 on, the carrying out of proper burial "in all woollen" may be mentioned. The cause of death is sometimes given (e.g. "hang'd herself"; "drowned"; "shot by soldier"; "killed on board vessel") and outbreaks of plague are frequently commented on.

The regulations governing the way in which registers were to be kept gradually became stricter. In 1711 an Act was passed ordering the keeping of proper register books with ruled and numbered pages. Worry about the growing number of illegal marriages led to the passing of Hardwicke's Act in 1754 "for the better preventing of clandestine marriages". Records were to be kept both of the reading of the banns (to make sure the couple were in fact free to marry) and of the marriage itself. From this date, marriage registers were kept separately from baptisms and burials, and details were filled in on printed forms, as shown in figure 17. These show whether the couple had been married before, and the parishes from which they came. The man's occupation is often given, and the signature or "mark" indicated whether they could write their own names.

In 1812, Rose's Act laid down that baptisms, marriages and burials should each be recorded in separate registers. Baptisms were to be recorded under column headings showing the parents' names, occupation and place of abode. Burial registers were to include the age and abode of the dead person. The registers were to be kept safely in a "dry well-painted iron chest".

For parishes where registers have been lost or destroyed, the Bishop's Transcripts may have survived. Each year the Churchwardens were required to send a transcript or copy of the registers to the Diocesan Registry. This was not always enforced and the transcripts are far from complete.

Growing numbers of non-conformists and non-churchgoers made a church-based system of registration increasingly unsatisfactory. In 1837, the registering of births, marriages and deaths became a civil affair, dealt with by registry offices. Church registers continued, but no longer had the same importance.

Gravestones in the parish churchyard can be used alongside the registers to piece together the fortunes of families who lived in the parish.

Where to Find Parish Registers

Most registers have now been transferred, with other parish records, to Record Offices. Parish catalogues usually give a full list of the registers from each parish. Registers kept in the parish may be seen with the Vicar's permission.

Bishop's Transcripts went to the Diocesan Registry, and are now with the Diocesan Records, usually in County Record Offices.

Questions Parish Registers Can Help to Answer

How many children were born to each family?

What were the most popular names?

What was the average age of death?

What changes can be seen in the pattern of births and deaths?

What was the literacy rate among men and women at different times?

From how far afield did people find their marriage partners?

18   Burial Register for the parish of St Thomas of the Cliffe, Lewes, Sussex, 1797.

▼

6
Quarter
Sessions Records

Between the government of king and parliament and the self-government of the parishes stood the authority of the county Justices of the Peace. They met four times a year at the Quarter Sessions, and were responsible for justice and administration within the county. In 1889, the administrative functions of Quarter Sessions passed to the newly-formed County Councils. Quarter Sessions carried on as courts of justice until 1974.

The office of Justice of the Peace originated in the fourteenth century. The Tudors relied heavily on their services, giving them the power to deal with almost all crimes, and responsibility for overseeing the work of Constables, Highways Surveyors and Overseers of the Poor. The Justices were unpaid but powerful. They were selected by the Lord Lieutenant of the county and most of them were country landowners, clergy, rich merchants or lawyers, whose wealth and status seemed to give them a natural right to office. They met at the Quarter Sessions ("our old talking shop", as one eighteenth-century Justice described it), to deal with the important business. "Petty Sessions" were also held in other parts of the county, in a special court-room, or even the local inn, and were attended by several Justices and a clerk. Minor matters were often dealt with by the individual Justice in his own front parlour or "justice room".

Quarter Sessions Records fall into the two main categories of justice and administration. There are also accounts, showing the money raised by the County Rate and how it was spent. The Clerk of the Peace was the legal adviser and the main administrator and some counties also appointed a County Treasurer. Items from Mr William Bullock's bill as Clerk of the Peace for the County of Essex in 1789 give some idea of the wide range of his responsibilities:

*For one Order appointing Mr. Samuel
Turtle to be Chief Constable* . . . .
*For entering the Indictments of false
Weights and Measures in a book kept for
that purpose* . . . .
*For one Order for Enrolling Consent of
Landowner and order of two Justices for
diverting an Highway at Terling in this
County* . . . .
*For drawing Resolutions of Court for
repairing the Shire House or building a
new one* . . . .
For drawing long and special Order concerning Act of Parliament lately passed . .
*For appointing a Committee to consider
what further Measures are necessary to be
taken for securing the Prisoners in and
preventing their Escape from out of the
Gaol* . . . .
*For one Order for the transportation of
George Sitler* . . . .
*For one Order adjudging Mary Toole to
be an incorrigible rogue* . . . .

▼

Essex } Newport House of Correction Kallendar, to and for
the Christmas quarter Sessⁿ Janʳʸ 1709 ———

Conveyed on
the 11ᵗʰ Novᵇʳ
1708, and
Publickly
Whipped in
the Town of
Waltham Holy
Cross and then
Dischᵈ ——

John Norman, Convicted of Grand Larceny, at the last
Michˢ quarter Sessⁿ octobʳ 8ᵗʰ 1708, was ordered to be
kept to hard Labour until the 11ᵗʰ of Novᵇʳ following, at
which time he was ordered to be Conveyed to Waltham
Holy Cross, and there publickly Whipped from the New
Inn to the Church, Between the Hours of 12 and one
oClock, and then Dischᵈ —————

Time Expired
and was Dischᵈ
the 18ᵗʰ Novᵇʳ
1708 ——

Peter Carroll Convicted of a Misdemeanor at the last —
Michˢ quarter Sessⁿ octobʳ 8ᵗʰ 1708, to be kept to hard
Labour for Six Weeks, and then to be Dischᵈ ———

Dischᵈ 9ᵗʰ
Novᵇʳ 1708,
having —
Satisfied
the penalty

George Moule of Saffron Walden Comᵈ 6ᵗʰ Novᵇʳ 1708, by Wᵐ
Gretton Clk:, to be Safely kept for three Months, being Convicted
upon the oath of John Chapman a Credible Witness, for that he
the said George Moule, not being a person by the Lawes of this
Realm qualified so to do, on the 11ᵗʰ Febʳ⁷ at Saffron Walden
aforesᵈ did keep and use an Engine for the destruction of the
Game called a Snare, Whereof he forfeited the Sum of five
pounds, And Whereas it duly appears upon the oath of
the Constable as otherwise, that he hath used his best —
Endeavour to Levy the said Sum on the Goods of the said
George Moule, but that no Sufficient distress Could be
found whereon to Levy the Same ——————

Time Expired
and was —
Dischᵈ the
5ᵗʰ Decᵇʳ
1708 ——

Ann Searle, a pauper of the poor House of Henham, Comᵈ
15ᵗʰ Novᵇʳ 1708, by Wᵐ Campbell Clk, to be Corrected and kept
to hard Labour for 21 days, being Convicted of refusing to —
Wear the Badge with a Large Roman P:, together with the
first Letter of the Name of the said parish, Contrary to the
Statute in that Case made and provided ———

Dischᵈ by the
same Justice
10ᵗʰ Janʳʸ

1709 ——

Mary Watson, a pauper of the poor House of Henham, Comᵈ
15ᵗʰ Novᵇʳ 1708, by Wᵐ Campbell Clk, to be safely kept until
she should be Dischᵈ by due Course of Law, being Convicted of
being a Rogue and Vagabond, for that she the said Mary
Watson having been before Convicted of being Idle and —
without Employment, and of being a Lewd and disorderly
Woman

The Quarter Sessions dealt with most crimes, but very serious offences were referred to the Assize Courts. Documents concerning each meeting of the Court of Quarter Sessions were put together into "Sessions Rolls", and the less formal paper documents were sometimes collected into "Sessions Bundles". All sorts of documents were included, from formal indictments to the highly personal, scrappily written and often amusing complaints and petitions of individuals.

Lists were kept of prisoners in the gaol or House of Correction. The Newport Calendar for 1789 (figure 19) gives details of each prisoner's offence and of the punishment to be given. Houses of Correction were set up from 1610 and were really meant for the "idle unemployed". This list includes Ann Searl, a pauper who refused to wear a badge

20 Information from Isaac Woods of Braintree in Essex about a theft of cloth, 1788. (Transcript on page 66)

▼

Essex. The Information of Isaac Woods of Braintree in the said County Bay Weaver taken upon Oath this 10th day of November 1788 before me Nicholas Wakeham D.D. One of his Majesty's Justices of the Peace in and for the said County.—

Who on his Oath saith That on Thursday night the 17th or Friday morning the 18th of July last past, the Weaving Shop of him the said Isaac Wood was broken open and about fifty Yards of Bays the property of Mr Joseph Savill were cut from the Loom and feloniously taken and carried away; And this Informant further saith That he hath seen several Pieces of Bays which he hath been informed were sold to divers Persons by one William Appleton late of Braintree aforesaid Weaver, and that the said Pieces of Bays are part of the Bays so cut and stolen from this Informant's Shop as aforesaid And this Informant further saith that between thirty and forty Pounds of Yarn the property of the said Joseph Savill were also at the same Time feloniously stolen taken & carried away from the said Shop; And further saith That he hath probable cause to suspect and doth Suspect that the said William Appleton and One Benjamin Usher (not yet taken) were the Persons who broke open the said Shop and feloniously took and carried away the said Bays and Yarn as aforesaid.—

Sworn the Day and year first above written before me

C V Wakeham

The mark of

Isaac † Wood

with the letter P showing the parish she came from, and Mary Watson, who was simply accused of being "idle and without employment" and of being a "lewd and disorderly woman". Other frequently mentioned crimes were poaching, theft and violence against neighbours. The usual punishments were public whipping, hard labour and fines, which could often not be paid.

Informations

These were informal written accounts given by witnesses and victims when a crime had taken place. They are often vividly written and the story usually loses nothing in the telling. The Information of Isaac Woods (figure 20) provides evidence concerning a theft of woven cloth, in order that William Appleton and Benjamin Usher could be charged with the offence.

Petitions

Justices of the Peace received many petitions asking them to show mercy towards prisoners, or to help those who had fallen on hard times. The petition of the poor prisoners in the County Gaol of Essex (figure 21) adopts the usual humble tone. It is not easy to read, but it is well worth the effort, as it gives a dramatic insight into how "lousy" prison life could be.

Indictments

These were the formal charges brought against individuals suspected of some wrongdoing. They were written on parchment and, since they were legal documents, Latin was used until 1733.

Presentments

These were informal accusations made by juries or individual Justices concerning minor offences or "Nuisances". The accused could be a parish which had failed to repair its roads and clear its ditches, or the keeper

21 Petition from the poor prisoners in the Essex County Gaol, 1674. (Transcript on page 65)

▼

of a disorderly ale-house. Parish Officers such as Constables and Highways Surveyors were often required to send "presentments" or reports to the Quarter Sessions concerning the general state of affairs in the parish.

Recognizances or Bonds

These ordered accused persons to appear at the Quarter Sessions or bound offenders over to future good behaviour.

Administration

Records of the Quarter Sessions' administrative activities may be found in the Order Books, which formally listed all the Court's proceedings, or in papers collected together under particular topics.

The upkeep of bridges was a county responsibility, and the county was also responsible for buildings, such as the Shire or County Hall, and the County Gaol. These were paid for from the County Rate, and looked after by the County Surveyor.

Roads were maintained by the parishes, but by the eighteenth century the upkeep of main roads had become too big a responsibility. Turnpike Trusts were set up to run the roads as a business, keeping them in good repair and charging travellers a toll to pass along them. The Quarter Sessions dealt with applications for the setting up of new Trusts or for the diversion of existing roads and footpaths.

Plans for public works and improvement schemes (canals, railways, gas, water, sewerage etc) had to be deposited with the Quarter Sessions.

The Quarter Sessions were also responsible for approving the appointments of Constables, Overseers of the Poor and Highways Surveyors. Ale-house keepers had to be licensed, charities and societies registered and the use of correct weights and measures enforced.

National concerns were also attended to. Acts of Parliament had to be implemented and registers of electors drawn up. Quarter Sessions Records also include returns concerning the collection of national taxes such as Hearth Tax. This was collected between 1662 and 1689 and involved the listing of all householders and the number of hearths in each house.

Where to Find Quarter Sessions Records

These are County Records and are therefore to be found in County Record Offices. Records of judicial proceedings can be found in Sessions "Rolls", "Bundles" or Order Books and are organized chronologically.

Administrative papers can often be found catalogued under subject headings (turnpikes, bridges, licensing of ale-houses etc) or in the Minute Books kept by Quarter Sessions committees.

Some Record Offices hold early County Council Records for the end of the nineteenth and the beginning of the twentieth centuries and some libraries also hold Council minutes.

Questions Quarter Sessions Records Can Help to Answer

What sorts of crimes were dealt with by the Quarter Sessions? (Informations, presentments)

How were offenders punished? (Calendars)

What were conditions like in gaols and Houses of Correction?

What did the County spend money on? (Clerk of the Peace and other accounts)

How and when were improvements made to roads, bridges, etc?

What do petitions to the Justices reveal about the problems of ordinary people? (Petitions)

7
Poor Law Records

Parish business was dominated by the huge and insoluble problem of what to do with the poor. Most of the money raised by the parish and much of the energy of its officers were directed towards poor relief in one form or another. The Quarter Sessions also had to deal with many aspects of the problem. The Justices were frequently petitioned by those who had fallen on hard times, and were called upon constantly to punish the offences of idleness and vagrancy. They also had to settle countless disputes between parishes about responsibility for paupers (people who were unable to support themselves).

The poor law system which operated until the nineteenth century was based on the Elizabethan Poor Law Act of 1601. Several householders in each parish were to be elected annually to help the Churchwardens as Overseers of the Poor. The poor of the parish were to be dealt with in three groups: the fit were to be set to work; the old and sick were to be housed and cared for, according to their needs; and the children were to be apprenticed. The Overseers were entitled to levy a rate on all parishioners to pay for the support of the poor.

The energies of the Overseers were divided between providing for the "deserving poor", and preventing unnecessary claims on the parish. Such claims were caused by vagrants from other parishes, by men who went off and left their families unsupported, and by women who gave birth to "bastard" children. A moral tone may have been adopted, but it was often the fear of financial liability which drove the Overseers into action. The extract from an Overseer's Account Book for 1747 (figure 22) shows the money and effort expended on getting a pregnant woman married, so that the parish would not be responsible for supporting her child.

Other entries in the Account Books show poor relief at work providing food, clothing, fuel and medical attention for those who needed it. Parishes often have records concerning charities and the distribution of "dole" money. Many of these charities were funded from gifts left in people's wills.

Poor relief was based on the two key principles of charity and correction. The giving of alms to the poor was a Christian duty, and this was practised in the building of almshouses, the endowment of numerous charities, and generosity towards the needy. On the other hand, idleness was a sin, to be punished and corrected, and it was for this purpose that Houses of Correction were set up.

Setting the poor to work, however, was no easy matter. From 1723, attempts were made to set up local workhouses where the poor could be housed and employed, or forfeit their right to poor relief. It was still often simpler, however, to help the poor to

◄ 22 Overseer of the Poor's Accounts for Glinton in Cambridgeshire (formerly Northamptonshire), 1747. (Transcript on page 63)

"husbandry", which meant that they became domestic servants or farm labourers. Children as young as nine were often apprenticed in this way and the apprenticeship indenture for Jane Wallet (figure 23) shows what was involved. Indentures were single documents on which several copies of an agreement were written and then cut apart along a wavy line. If there was later a dispute, the parts could be fitted together again to prove that those who signed them had accepted the same agreement. This agreement was drawn up between Jane Wallet ("advised and assisted" by the Overseers of the Poor) and John Hood, a farmer, who was to become her master. She promised to serve him and his family faithfully and obediently until the age of 21. He, in return for a down payment of £5 by the parish, agreed to feed and clothe her, and to teach her "the Art of Housewifery". Apprenticeship "bonds" often accompanied these indentures. In these, the new master promised that, from now on, the Churchwardens, Overseers and parishioners would be caused no further expense by the apprenticed child.

Until the mid-seventeenth century, the poor were able to seek employment wherever it could be found. Parishes, however, did not welcome paupers from elsewhere, who could not contribute to the parish rates; so the laws concerning "settlement" (the right to settle in other than your home parish) were tightened up.

Punitive measures were also taken to cope with the rising tides of vagrancy and illegitimacy. In 1743, three classes of vagrants were defined: "idle and disorderly persons";

carry on with their own work and to provide them with payments in money or in kind. Yet this did little to discourage pauperism, and the expenditure on poor relief continued to soar.

The best way of making sure that orphans and the children of parents who could not afford to support them caused no expense to the parish was to apprentice them out. Some children were taught trades, but most were apprenticed to learn "housewifery" or

23 Jane Wallet's Apprenticeship Indenture, from ►
Cowbit in Lincolnshire, 1727. (Transcript on page 61)

This Indenture Witnesseth That Jane Catlet pauper being fatherless and Motherless and Wholly provided for by y.e parish of Cowbit in the County of Lincoln Doth by the advice & Assistance of John Bramsby Churchwarden & John Cock & Henry Stevenson Overseers of the poor of the s.d parish put & place herself Apprentice to John Hood of Moulton in the s.d County of Lincoln farmer with him to dwell & Serve from the date of these p.sents until she shall Accomplish her full Age of One and Twenty years during which Terme the s.d Apprentice her s.d Master faithfully shall Serve in all Lawfull business According to her power Wit and Ability and honestly Orderly & Obediently in all things demean and behave herself towards her s.d Master & all his during the s.d Terme And the s.d John Hood for himself his Ex.ors Adm.ors & Assignes in Consideration of the Summ of Five pounds of of lawful money of Great Brittain to him in hand p.d by the parishioners of Cowbitt aforesd the Rec.t whereof he doth hereby Acknowledge) doth Cov.t & grant to & with the said Churchwardens and Overseers & every of them & their Successors for the Time being by these p.sents That he or they the s.d Apprentice in the Art of Housewifery shall & will teach & instruct and also shall & will during the s.d Terme find and allow unto the s.d Apprentice meet Competent & Sufficient Meat Drink & Apparel Lodging Washing & all other things Necessary & fitt for an Apprentice And also shall & will so provide for the s.d Apprentice that she be not any way a Charge to the s.d parish & parishioners of the same but of & from all Charge shall & will save y.e s.d parish & parishioners harmless and indemnified during the s.d Terme And at the end of the s.d Terme shall & will make provide allow & deliver unto the s.d Apprentice double Apparel of all sorts good & New (that is to say) a good new Suit for the holy days and another for the Working Days In Witness whereof the parties aforesaid to these p.sent Indentures Interchangably have put their hands & Seals this Fourteenth day of March Anno Dni 1726/7

Sealed & Delivered (being legally Stampt)   John Hood
in the p.sence of us
                    H. Everard
                    W. Edwards

29

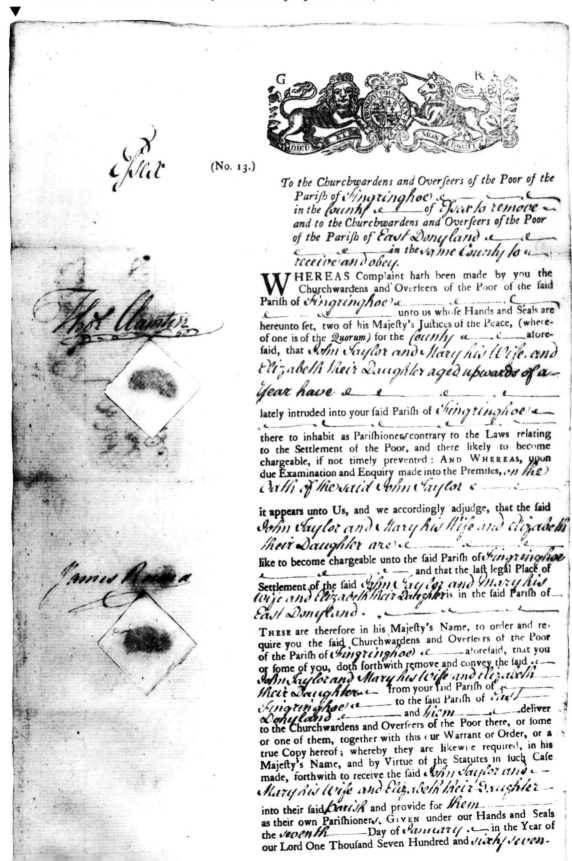

(No. 13.)

To the Churchwardens and Overseers of the Poor of the Parish of *Fingringhoe* in the County of *Essex* to remove and to the Churchwardens and Overseers of the Poor of the Parish of *East Donyland* in the same County to receive and obey.

WHEREAS Complaint hath been made by you the Churchwardens and Overseers of the Poor of the said Parish of *Fingringhoe* unto us whose Hands and Seals are hereunto set, two of his Majesty's Justices of the Peace, (whereof one is of the *Quorum*) for the County aforesaid, that *John Taylor and Mary his Wife and Elizabeth their Daughter aged upwards of a Year* have lately intruded into your said Parish of *Fingringhoe* there to inhabit as Parishioners contrary to the Laws relating to the Settlement of the Poor, and there likely to become chargeable, if not timely prevented: AND WHEREAS, upon due Examination and Enquiry made into the Premises, *on the Oath of the said John Taylor* it appears unto Us, and we accordingly adjudge, that the said *John Taylor and Mary his Wife and Elizabeth their Daughter are* like to become chargeable unto the said Parish of *Fingringhoe* and that the last legal Place of Settlement of the said *John Taylor and Mary his Wife and Elizabeth their Daughter* is in the said Parish of *East Donyland.*

THESE are therefore in his Majesty's Name, to order and require you the said Churchwardens and Overseers of the Poor of the Parish of *Fingringhoe* aforesaid, that you or some of you, doth forthwith remove and convey the said *John Taylor and Mary his Wife and Elizabeth their Daughter* from your said Parish of *Fingringhoe* to the said Parish of *East Donyland* and them deliver to the Churchwardens and Overseers of the Poor there, or some or one of them, together with this our Warrant or Order, or a true Copy hereof; whereby they are likewise required, in his Majesty's Name, and by Virtue of the Statutes in such Case made, forthwith to receive the said *John Taylor and Mary his Wife and Elizabeth their Daughter* into their said *Parish* and provide for *them* as their own Parishioners. GIVEN under our Hands and Seals the *seventh* Day of *January* in the Year of our Lord One Thousand Seven Hundred and *sixty seven*.

"rogues and vagabonds"; and "incorrigible rogues". Public whipping was the general punishment for vagrants, for "lewd women" who produced bastards, and even for paupers who resisted the indignity of wearing the compulsory badge with its large letter P.

Settlement certificates, settlement examinations and removal orders make up the bulk of Poor Relief Records. Settlement certificates were needed to establish the right to live in a parish. Examinations were enquiries into a person's lawful "place of settlement". Removal orders sent people back to their parish of origin.

The removal order in figure 24 ordered John Taylor, with his wife and baby daughter, to return to their last legal place of settlement. It was issued by the Justices, in response to a complaint from the Overseers in Fingringhoe, where they had attempted to settle. The printed format indicates that it was routine business, but it was an unhappy process for the people involved. They were given a pass, but were liable to be harassed on the journey and were probably less than welcome in the parish to which they returned.

The inadequate and overburdened system of parish-based poor relief came to an end with the Poor Law Amendment Act of 1834. Under the central authority of the Poor Law Commissioners, parishes were joined into "unions", which set up workhouses for each area under local boards of "Guardians". Parish charities continued, but, for many people, poor relief now meant banishment to the dreaded workhouse. Registers and minute books kept by the Boards of Guardians give a detailed picture of how these institutions were run.

Where to Find Poor Law Records

Overseers' of the Poor accounts, settlement certificates, removal orders, apprenticeship indentures and charity papers are all Parish Records, which have now usually been deposited in the Record Office. A full list of what is available will be catalogued with other Parish Records, under the name of the parish.

Petitions, presentments, indictments and calendars of prisoners contain many references to the problems of poverty and can be found among Quarter Sessions Records in the Record Office.

Workhouse registers and minutes kept by the Boards of Guardians have also been deposited in Record Offices.

Questions Poor Law Records Can Help to Answer

Where did vagrants come from and was their settlement resisted? (Settlement papers)

How were paupers treated in workhouses and Houses of Correction? (Quarter Sessions Records and records of Boards of Guardians)

What "crimes" were paupers punished for? (Quarter Sessions Records)

What charities did the parish have and how were they used? (Charity papers)

What did the Overseers of the Poor do? (Overseers' Accounts)

Who were pauper children apprenticed to and under what conditions? (Apprenticeship indentures)

8
Borough Records

Local government until the late nineteenth century was made up of the three separate systems of the parish, the county and the borough. A "borough" was a town which had been granted privileges of self-government by royal charter. Many of these ancient boroughs were given charters during the Middle Ages, and few were created later than the seventeenth century. The ruling body in the borough was known as the "Corporation", but as they were all set up at different times and under different circumstances, their constitutions varied widely.

Boroughs had the right to hold their own courts, to deal with civil and some criminal matters, and Justices were often appointed from the Corporation. In many respects, Borough Records are similar to those of the parish and Quarter Sessions, but some go back even further in time. Records were kept in a special chest in the Town or Guild Hall and may include original charters and records relating to the borough courts, the Mayor and Corporation and the Town Clerk. The interests of merchants and tradesmen are reflected in records concerning apprentices and the merchant guilds.

As towns expanded, pressing needs developed with which local government had no means of coping. In order to bring gas to a town, or to improve the water supply, Improvement Commissioners were appointed, private Bills were passed through Parliament and companies were set up to carry out the work. The Act for bringing gas lighting to Leicester (figure 25) is an example of many hundreds of separate Acts which were passed at the end of the eighteenth and the beginning of the nineteenth centuries in order to improve conditions in towns. It was difficult to co-ordinate these improvements, however, and it was quite likely that, as soon as the streets had been paved, they would be ripped up again for the laying on of gas and then for new sewers, and so it went on.

In 1835, the government of boroughs was reformed by the Municipal Corporations Act. Councillors were to be fairly elected by the ratepayers, justice was separated from administration and, for the first time, the powers of borough councils were clearly defined. Responsibility for "paving, lighting, cleansing, watching, regulating, supplying with water and improving" the borough was now to be taken over by the reformed Corporations.

As a result of the Municipal Corporations Act, many of the small old boroughs lost their independence. During the nineteenth century, towns, such as Manchester and Birmingham, which were now very large, became boroughs for the first time. The Local Government Acts of 1888 and 1894 established a comprehensive system of county borough councils, which operated independently from the newly-formed county councils.

Where to Find Borough Records

Records were kept by the old boroughs in special "muniments rooms". Some large boroughs now have their own Record Office, which may be in the library or civic centre, but many others have deposited their records in County Record Offices.

The Local Government Acts at the end of the nineteenth century led to the publication of council minutes. Developments in health, housing, education, etc, can be traced in these council committee minutes which have been deposited in Record Offices and public libraries.

Questions Borough Records Can Help to Answer

When was the borough "incorporated" and what privileges were given to it by its charters?

Who held office in the borough and what did they do?

How was the borough affected by changes in the organization of local government during the nineteenth century?

What action in areas such as health, housing and education is recorded in council minutes from the end of the nineteenth century?

How and when did improvements such as gas, water, paving, etc, take place?

ANNO PRIMO & SECUNDO

GEORGII IV. REGIS.

****

Cap. iii.

An Act for lighting with Gas the Borough of *Leicester*, in the County of *Leicester*, and the Liberties, Precincts, and Suburbs thereof.
[24th *March* 1821.]

WHEREAS the Borough of *Leicester*, in the County of *Leicester*, with the Suburbs and Vicinity thereof, is large and populous, and it would be a great Advantage to the Inhabitants thereof and to the Public at large, if the Streets and other public Roads, Ways, Passages, Lanes, and Places therein, were better lighted : And whereas Inflammable Air, Coke, Oil, Tar, Pitch, Asphaltum, Ammoniacal Liquor, and Essential Oil, may be procured from Coal ; and Inflammable Air may also be procured from other Substances : And whereas the said Inflammable Air, being conveyed by means of Pipes, may be safely and beneficially used for lighting the several Roads, Streets, Squares, Market Places, Ways, Lanes, and other Places within the said Borough, and the Parishes of *Saint Margaret, Saint Mary,* and *Saint Leonard, The Bishops Fee, The New-arke, The Castle View, The Friars, The Abbey Gate, The Wood Gate* (the Suburbs of the said Borough), and other Places near or adjoining thereto, and for lighting private Houses, Shops, Warehouses, Manufactories, and other Buildings, and the Coke may be beneficially employed as Fuel in private Houses and Manufactories ; and the said Oil, Tar, Pitch, Asphaltum, Ammoniacal Liquor, and Essential Oil, may be used and employed in various other ways, with Safety

[*Local.*]   M   and

▲

25   Act of Parliament for lighting Leicester with gas, 1821.

9
Maps

Maps provide a fascinating record of continuity and change in local communities. Most maps were designed with a specific purpose in mind and are therefore selective in what they show, but many different types of maps are available for most areas, from the eighteenth century onwards, and from them it is possible to piece together a wealth of information.

Estate Maps

Manorial surveys in the Middle Ages relied on words rather than maps, but by the seventeenth century, country landowners were taking an increasing interest in the charting of their estates and were employing surveyors to make maps for them. Map-making now developed from rough-and-ready picture-making, such as in the example on the front cover, into a sophisticated skill reflecting new interest in mathematics and accurate scientific recording. Estate-owners wanted maps which would delight the eye as well as inform the mind, and in the eighteenth century, maps were embellished with decorative titles and compass points and were often delicately coloured or inset with local scenes.

Although many such maps were produced, they do not add up to a uniform pattern of national coverage. They reflect the land-owner's pride and interest in his estates, and show roads, natural features and above all fields, rather than the layout of villages and towns.

Town Plans

There had always been an interest in the mapping of towns, though these maps were often "prospects", or elevated views, showing the beauty or grandeur of the town and its daily life, rather than its exact dimensions. Many such early maps exist, particularly of London. The seventeenth century brought a greater concern for exactness and the attempt at a more comprehensive approach to the mapping of the country as a whole.

In 1579, Christopher Saxton produced *An Atlas of England and Wales*, consisting of a complete collection of County maps. Then in 1612, John Speed produced the first real collection of urban maps, including seventy-three town plans as insets to County maps, in *The Theatre of the Empire of Great Britaine*. Throughout the eighteenth century many town plans continued to be produced as insets to County maps, not on individual sheets but in bound volumes. The plan of Colchester (figure 26) (technically, a plan is a map on a sufficiently large scale to show all the main features) was published in 1777. It is beautifully engraved, and the treatment

26   Town Plan of Colchester in Essex by André and Chapman, 1777.

of fields, windmills and trees (with shadows) shows a continuing concern to make a picture, rather than a pure mathematical drawing. Nevertheless, map-making skills had come a long way, and by the nineteenth century the two-dimensional map, precisely drawn to a consistent scale, was firmly established.

Improvement Plans

The boom in canal-building in the late eighteenth century started a new form of specialist map-making. For a bill to build a canal to be passed through Parliament, a map had to be drawn up to show the route of the proposed canal or river-navigation and the area through which it was to pass. Nineteenth-century railway construction demanded a similar procedure. The progress of the proposed railway line through town and countryside was drawn out, together with the fields and buildings on either side. These were numbered and described in a "book of reference", which went with the map. Several copies were made of each map, and one was deposited with the local Clerk of the Peace. As a result, many Record Offices now have large collections of such plans, though, as with canals, far more railways were planned than were ever built.

As the nineteenth century progressed, plans were drawn up to illustrate every proposed improvement scheme: gas-lighting, sewerage, water-supply, road-building, housing development and so on. These plans were carefully drawn and were functional rather than decorative. They served the same purpose as plans being drawn up in council offices across the country today, which will, in turn, become records to be studied by future generations.

Enclosure and Tithe Award Maps

The Enclosure and Tithe Maps are the most detailed maps in existence for many parishes, before the making of large-scale Ordnance Survey maps. The enclosure of land in the interests of more efficient farming had been going on for centuries, creating the patchwork of small hedged fields which now typifies the English countryside. Early enclosure often took place by private arrangement and left few records. In the century from 1760, a major "finishing off" process took place. Some parishes, particularly in the Midlands, were now converted for the first time from the shared open-field system. In many parishes new Enclosure Acts were drawn up to enclose the remaining areas of open common and wasteland.

From 1801 a series of General Enclosure Acts streamlined the process of enclosure (or "inclosure" as it was called by the lawyers). The enclosure documents consisted of a printed Act of Parliament, authorising the enclosure, and the Enclosure Award itself. This was generally handwritten on parchment, in book or roll form, and was a lengthy document, describing the size and ownership of the new fields and the position of roads etc, as in figure 27. It was accompanied by a large-scale map, on which fields were correspondingly numbered, and roads and buildings were also marked. Information is often given about earlier enclosures, and sometimes even about the old open-field arrangement. A typical enclosure map (much reduced in size) is shown in figure 28.

Two copies of the Enclosure Award were required. One went to the Clerk of the Peace, for the County, and one to the parish chest. Many are now in local Record Offices. The maps are usually large, but they can be traced, with care, and some Record Offices have made photographic reductions.

Tithe Award maps were the result of the Tithe Commutation Act of 1836 and most were drawn up in the 1840s. They provide

27   Enclosure Award for Great and Little Chishill in Essex, 1818. (Transcript on page 63)

▼

▲ 28   Enclosure Award Map for Great and Little Chishill in Essex, 1818.

similar information to enclosure maps and there is a good chance that one or both types of map can be found for a particular parish.

Traditionally, the Vicar or "incumbent" of a parish had the right to one-tenth (a tithe) of all the produce of the land, since it was the duty of Christians to support the church. "Tithe barns" still exist in some villages, into which tithes of corn and other produce were collected. It was the responsibility of the Vicar or tithe-owner (rights were often sold off to wealthy

"impropriators") to collect their own tithes from the fields, and this caused endless disputes and much resentment. Reform came in 1836, with the replacement of tithes in kind with fixed money payments. These were calculated by Tithe Commissioners, on the basis of average corn prices for the previous seven years. Almost three-quarters of England and Wales was surveyed by

37

Commissioners, in order to fix money-rents for each piece of land on a fair basis. The Tithe Award for each parish consisted of a detailed map, showing numbered fields and buildings, and an "apportionment", which was drawn up on a printed form (a section of one is shown in figure 29). This had columns for the ownership, tenancy, state of cultivation (wood, arable, pasture, homestead, etc) and size of each plot, and showed the amount of rent-charge to be paid instead of tithes.

Three copies had to be made of each Tithe Award: one to be deposited with the Tithe Commissioners in London; one with the Diocesan Registry; and one to be kept in the parish chest.

Ordnance Survey Maps

Increased interest in map-making and a concern for better overall national coverage led to the creation of the Ordnance Survey in 1791. Work began on a 1"-to-1-mile series of maps covering the whole country, which was published between 1805 and 1873. By the end of the nineteenth century complete series of 6"-to-1-mile and 25"-to-1-

mile maps had been produced. The 25" maps show all buildings and are widely available in Record Offices. They are an ideal starting-point for making comparisons with earlier and later maps.

Work has gone on throughout the twentieth century on new editions of 1", 6" and 25" maps (and now their metric equivalents). Available for every part of the country, Ordnance Survey maps are of prime importance in showing the development of local communities over the last hundred years.

Where to Find Maps

Estate Maps are usually in Record Offices, unless in private ownership, and are catalogued under place or name of landowner. Town Plans can be found in County or Borough Record Offices. Libraries often have very good collections, including facsimiles of early maps. Some originals may be found in Town Halls.

29 Apportionment accompanying Tithe Award Map for Brookfield in Essex, 1846.

▼

Numbers referring to the Plan.	NAME AND DESCRIPTION of LANDS AND PREMISES.	STATE of CULTIVATION.	QUANTITIES IN STATUTE MEASURE.			Amount of Rent-Charge apportioned upon the several Lands, and to whom payable.					
						PAYABLE TO VICAR.			PAYABLE TO *Impropriators*		
			A.	R.	P.	£.	s.	d.	£.	s.	d.
		Brought forward	226	2	2				84	4	3
121	*Some field*	*Ara*	16	2	14				6	10	
122	*Little Glove House Shots*	*Ara*	9	2	6				3	13	
123	*Homestead*		4		8				2		6
124	*Broom pightle*	*Pas*	4	2	12				1	1	9
125	*...*	*...*	8		7				2	2	1
126	*Further Glove House Shots*	*Ara*	7	1	23				2	19	-
124	*Middle D°*	*Ara*	10	3	36				4	6	6
147	*Earl of Bonnards Field*	*Ara* { *Pasto*	12	2	13				4	9	6
					32						3
292	*The marsh*	*Pas*	11	1	6				2	13	7
293	*North meadow*	*Pas*	10	1	36				2	9	7
			322	1	14				116	12	

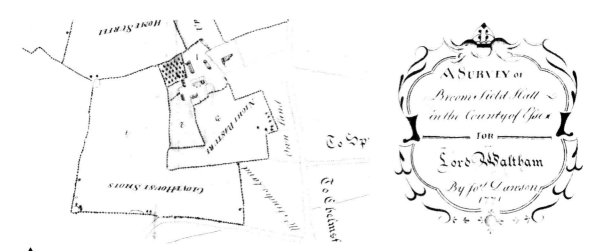

▲
30   Estate Map showing Broomfield in Essex, 1771.

31   Tithe Award Map for Broomfield, 1846.
▼

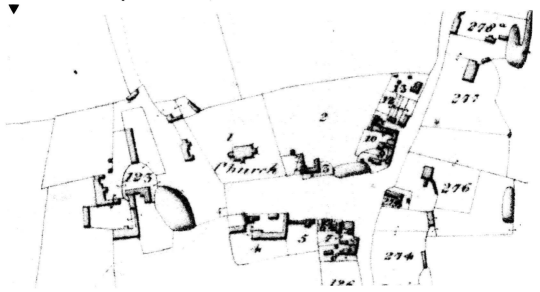

32   25″ Ordnance Survey Map for Broomfield,
1897.
▼

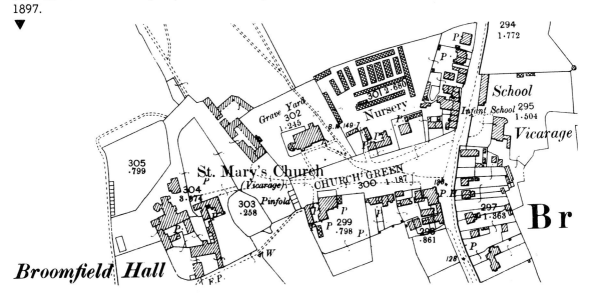

Improvement Plans can be found by looking in the place or subject index ("railways", etc) or under Quarter Sessions or Council Papers in the Record Office. Later plans may still be held by council departments.

Enclosure Awards are usually found in Record Offices. Tithe Awards can be found in the Record Office, among Parish or Diocesan Records.

Ordnance Survey Maps can be found in Record Offices, which usually have the best sets of earlier maps, but libraries also hold good collections. Enquire at a local Ordnance Survey Office for up-to-date information about the maps available now.

Questions Maps Can Help to Answer

How was the land divided up into fields?

How did a town or village grow between two points in time?

Who were the main landowners?

How did the conventions of map-making develop?

How was the land used (arable, pasture, waste, etc)?

To what extent have major features (roads, etc) remained the same?

10
Inventories and Wills

Inventories

In 1529 it became law that, when a person died, his house must be visited and all his possessions listed and valued before the instructions in his will could be carried out. This list, called a "probate inventory", was then sent to a church court where the will was "proved" and made official. This practice lasted from Tudor to Victorian times, though most surviving inventories date from the period 1550 to 1750. The seventeenth century is particularly well-covered.

The inventory was usually drawn up by respectable neighbours, who needed to be able to write and to add up sums. These valuers walked round the house, going from room to room and listing everything they saw as they went. As a result, inventories are rather like guided tours of the houses in which they were made. They describe the layout of rooms and how they were furnished, and how much each item was worth.

Many people worked at home in work-shops or "shops" which were part of the house, so the tools of their trades are included. Even in towns, people grew much of their own food, and there is often a long list of crops, animals and farming implements found "in the field" and "in the yard". Utensils for making beer, butter or cheese could be found in the kitchen, buttery or outhouse, and upstairs rooms often contained items such as spinning wheels and sacks of grain, as well as beds.

From these inventories, a remarkably clear picture of life in the seventeenth and eighteenth centuries emerges. The homeless left no record, but there are many short inventories, totalling just a few pounds, which show how the poor lived. Other inventories stretch over several pages, revealing the lives of the rich and the luxuries they enjoyed. Inventories also show how items such as clocks, mirrors and books, at first found only in richer homes, gradually became more common.

The inventory in figure 33 shows a fairly typical list of possessions for a reasonably well-off craftsman at the end of the seventeenth century. Most inventories are laid out in a similar way, with the sections usually in this order.

Lots of words were used in inventories which we no longer use today, and these vary from one part of the country to the other. This is particularly true of names for equipment used for cooking over an open fire, and of names used for farm animals. The short glossary on page 43 gives the meanings of words used in figure 33.

33 Inventory of the goods of Robert Bee of
Harmston in the County of Lincoln, 1696.
(Transcript on page 64)

1. Standard formal beginning, giving name, place, trade and date.

2. Value of money and clothing.

3. The contents of the house listed room by room, giving value of each item in pounds, shillings and pence.

4. The contents of the workshop.

5. The contents of outhouses (brewing equipment, etc).

6. Crops, animals and farming equipment kept in the yard outside the house, and on land owned by the dead person.

7. An allowance for anything which may have been left out.

8. TOTAL VALUE

9. Signatures of valuers.

goods and chattels — movable possessions.

Imp (rimis) — first ("Item" introduces each subsequent unit in the list).

pewter — shiny grey metal used for plates, bowls, mugs, etc.

fire-irons — metal implements used with an open fire.

buttery — cool store-room.

tow wheel — wheel for spinning coarse yarn.

bacon-flitch — smoked and salted side of pig, kept hanging up to provide meat through the winter.

warp — threads stretched lengthwise on loom.

strike — a level measure (of grain, etc).

cratch — rack for holding animal food out of doors.

Wills

A will shows what a man possessed (until 1882 women rarely made wills unless they were spinsters or widows), and how he wanted it shared out between his friends and relations after his death. It often shows how well he got on with the various members of his family, and the importance which he attached to particular possessions. Sometimes the most valuable gifts which he had to give away were "my best suit" or "my best bedstead", but these were gratefully received by the next generation.

Most wills start formally: "I bequeath

34　The Will of Sarah Abearne of Irchester, Northamptonshire, 1703. (Transcript on page 61)

▼

my soul into the hands of Almighty God . . . and my body to be buried in the churchyard". Many end with a sum of money "for the poor of the parish". In between, there is usually a wealth of detail, making the intentions of the writer in this important last act absolutely clear. Sarah Abearne was a poor widow. She was able to sign the will (figure 34) herself, but she got someone else to write it for her. It uses the normal legal phrases, but there was not a lot to give away. (The inventory made after her death in 1727 valued the whole contents of her house at just £14.) She leaves a token shilling to her son, and everything else to her daughter Bridgitt who, as "executor" of the will, was responsible for seeing that it was carried out.

John Clifton (part of whose diary appears on page 59) took a far more detailed interest in what was to become of his worldly goods after his death. He had already made a will, but the afterthought or "Codicil" (figure 35) was added two years before he died. It is in his own handwriting and he clearly takes great delight in setting out the full list of goods at his disposal. The part shown gives many details about the house and its furnishings, and about John Clifton's interests and style of life. He goes on to list the tools of his trade, and numerous books, maps and political magazines. The whole will conjures up a vivid impression of this Northamptonshire joiner and his pride in being an all-round man of his times.

In cases where no will had been made, a "bond of administration" was issued by the church court. This appointed an executor who undertook to act fairly in disposing of the dead person's property and to present an account of what had been done.

From 1858, Probate Registries were set up all over the country, under the authority of the Principal Probate Registry at Somerset House in London. Probate, the official approving of wills, ceased to be the responsibility of the church, and inventories were no longer needed.

Where to Find Inventories and Wills

Until the 1857 Court of Probate Act, inventories and wills were deposited in Diocesan Registries. Most have now been transferred, with other Diocesan Records, to County Record Offices.

In most Record Offices, inventories and wills are catalogued by the name of the person or by the date. The parish and the person's trade also usually appear in the catalogue, so it is possible to select an inventory or will by person, place, trade or period of time.

Some Record Offices hold printed collections of inventories. In many parts of the country, Record Offices hold "glossaries", which give the meanings of dialect words and technical terms appearing in local inventories. *The English Dialect Dictionary* can often be found in libraries, but an ordinary large English dictionary is sufficient for solving many problems.

Questions Inventories Can Help to Answer

What rooms did a house contain, and how were they furnished?

What food could people provide for themselves?

What work was done at home?

Can family relationships be worked out from wills?

How wide was the difference between the possessions of rich and poor?

How do the houses in inventories of a particular date compare with modern houses?

35   Codicil to the Will of John Clifton of Oundle, Northamptonshire, 1783. (Transcript on page 62)

▼

11
School Records

Log-books

Until Victorian times there were no state schools and the main provider of education was the church. In 1811 the National Society was set up by the Church of England, to extend elementary education and provide more children with basic Christian instruction. Many "National Schools" were started in the 1840s, catering for children from the age of two or three until they left school at eleven or twelve.

In the mid-nineteenth century, the government began to provide money to support existing schools and to make education more widely available. It now became necessary to keep a check on how this money was being spent. From 1862, every school which received a government grant was instructed to keep a "log-book". This was a school diary kept by the Master or Mistress in charge, which could be read later by Inspectors or Managers.

In 1870 the Education Act began the setting up of "Board Schools" to fill the remaining gaps in what was to become a national system of free, compulsory education for all children. From now on, the regulations governing schools became stricter.

36   Log-book entry from Glinton School, Cambridgeshire (formerly Northamptonshire), 1886.

In 1894, the New Code laid down clear rules about the keeping of log-books.

The log-book must be stoutly bound, and contain not less than 300 ruled pages. It must be kept by the principal teacher, who is required to enter in it from time to time such events as the introduction of new books, apparatus, or courses of instruction, any plan of lessons approved by the Inspector, the visits of managers, absence, illness, or failure of duty on the part of any of the school staff, or any special circumstances affecting the school.

The page from a log-book written in the spring of 1886 (figure 36) gives a typical account of school life with children being absent, parents being difficult, visitors calling, accidents happening . . . .

Inspectors carried out an annual inspection, examining the children in basic subjects and commenting on how well the school was doing. Their reports had to be copied word-for-word into the log-book, and they sometimes give a rather different picture of the school's achievements from the Head's day-to-day comments!

The Inspector's report in figure 37 indicates the subjects being covered and how well the children were being taught. Teachers and children usually grew equally anxious as the day of the inspection approached. This was not helped by the system of payment by results, which meant, as in this case, that the grant was reduced if the school did badly. The list of staff shows that the Master had a difficult task, aided only by a young Pupil Teacher who had stayed on at the school and was learning as she went along, and an "Article 84" teacher who had been approved as responsible and respectable, but who was otherwise unqualified.

Log-books can be very revealing about the life of a school. They often show the Master or Mistress in despair over poor attendance, which meant less money for the school, and in difficulty getting the children up to standard for the government inspection. Laws on truancy were gradually tightened up, but log-books constantly complain about children being absent for reasons ranging from "heavy snow", "hot weather" and "harvesting", to "Baptist Sunday School tea" and "wild beast show".

Log-books also record how schools changed over the years, with alterations in buildings and teaching staff and the introduction of new equipment and teaching methods. The curriculum is often shown in the form of a detailed syllabus for the coming year, making clear what children of different ages were expected to learn. Head

Teachers still keep log-books today, and these will be of as much interest to future generations as those from a century ago are to us now.

Punishment Books

Teachers were expected to keep strict discipline. This meant the routine punishment of children for a host of small crimes such as "lateness", "inattention", "talking", "getting ink on book" or "going into girls' yard". When a child was caned, the teacher in charge had to keep a record of the offence, and of the punishment. The punishment book gives a good indication of how children were expected to behave and of what they actually got up to. In some books the same names crop up again and again, giving the impression of teachers at their wits' end about how to bring their "insubordinate" charges under control. The page from a punishment book (figure 38) shows a typical assortment of minor offences, and one major confrontation between teacher and pupil.

37   Inspector's Report from the log-book of Glinton School, Cambridgeshire (formerly Northamptonshire), 1886.

▼

Registers

The name, age and address of every child who entered school were recorded on the "Admission Register", and the date and reason for withdrawal was added when the child left. These registers can be very useful for tracing local families and for identifying people on old school photographs.

Class registers were filled in every day with great care, as the school's grant was based on average attendance figures. The 1875 girls' class register (figure 39) is laid out very like a modern school register. The absence symbols used were "a" for absent, "s" for sick, "w" for weather and "h" for needed at home. It is clear that many children attended very infrequently, and registers like this usually show a dramatic thinning-out as summer and harvest approached.

Secondary Schools

State secondary schools developed out of the elementary school system from the end of the nineteenth century and produced similar records. The old grammar schools have a far longer history and there were many hundreds in existence by the end of the seventeenth century. They were supported by endowments (gifts which continued to provide money over a long period), and by the payment of fees. Such schools were often under the control of the church or sometimes of the borough. Some of these schools have been incorporated into the state system, but many are now fully independent day or boarding schools. Surviving records may include original foundation charters, old registers listing past and present pupils, and miscellaneous items such as timetables and even exercise books.

Where to Find School Records

School log-books first became compulsory in 1862 for schools receiving a government grant. Few remain from quite as early as this, but many date from the 1880s and 1890s. The log-books, punishment books, registers and other records of many schools have been deposited in Record Offices and

38   Punishment Book from Newborough School, Cambridgeshire, 1910.

No.	Name	Offence	Date of Offence	Punishment Awarded	Date of Punishment.	Remarks	Initials of Manager, Clerk, or Inspector
		January 1910					
	Ernest Adams	Breaking a peg	Jan 10	2 strokes	Jan 10		
	John Sutton	Throwing water	" 10	3 "	Jan 10		
	George Thompson	at each other	" 10	3 "	" 10		
	Elsie Ship	Putting ink on	" 11	1 "	" 11	First offence	
	Edith Stacey	each others books	11	1 "	" 11	" "	
	Mary Lane	Refusal to obey: insolence to teachers. Kicking teacher Snatching cane away & breaking it	" 17	Perhaps from 12 to 15 strokes on the back and shoulders	" 17	This was the worst insubordination I have ever met with	
	Charles Sutton	Talking	" 20	2 strokes	Jan 20		
	John Cox	Getting ink on books	" "	2 "	"		
	Arthur Vickers	Went into girls yard	" 26	3 "	" 26		
	James Cave	Talking	" 28	1 stroke	" 28		

this is particularly likely if the school has merged, moved site, or gone out of existence. The records of other schools have remained in the school, under the care of the Head Teacher. It is often possible for schools to borrow back log-books, etc, which have been deposited in Record Offices, so it is always worth approaching the Head Teacher first.

Secondary school records are usually of more recent origin. Record Offices hold the records of School Boards and sometimes the early records of Council Education Departments, and these can be useful in tracing the development of local state education.

Records from some of the endowed grammar schools can be found amongst Borough or Diocesan Records in the Record Office. Long-established public schools often hold substantial record collections of their own.

Background information about schools and their histories can be gained from directories, and from the Victoria County Histories, which are widely available in Record Offices and reference libraries.

Questions School Records Can Help to Answer

When was the school founded and for what purpose?

Who were the staff, and what were their qualifications?

How good was the attendance, and what were the reasons for absence?

How was discipline maintained?

What subjects were taught and by what methods?

How was the school affected by national events (e.g. the two world wars)?

Have any families attended the school over several generations? How has it changed in that time?

39　Girls' Class Register from Huttoft in Lincolnshire, 1875.
▼

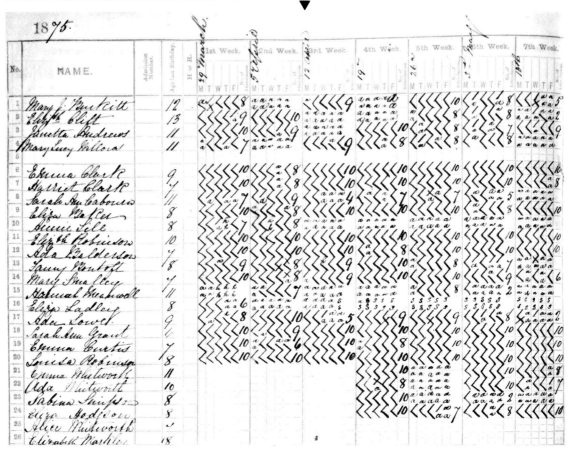

12
Census Records

Until the beginning of the nineteenth century, no-one really knew how large the population was. Parish Registers gave some clues, and parishes and towns often drew up their own lists for the purpose of collecting taxes or rates, but these never added up to a complete national picture. Many people were suspicious about the very idea of a census, thinking that it could give away national secrets, but during the late eighteenth century there was much anxious discussion about the relationship between the economy and the size of the population. Accurate statistics showing how many people the country was supporting and how fast this number was growing were clearly needed.

The first census was held in 1801, with the intention of gaining broad statistical information, rather than gathering details about individual households. Parish officials acted as "Enumerators", sending in the total number of people living in each parish. A population size of just over nine million was calculated, though this was probably an underestimate.

From then on, censuses were carried out regularly every ten years, as they still are

40   The questions asked at censuses during the nineteenth century. *Up to 1831, only the broad category of Family Occupation was recorded.
▼

	1801	1811	1821	1831	1841	1851	1861	1871	1881	1891
Name					✓	✓	✓	✓	✓	✓
Sex	✓	✓	✓	✓	✓	✓	✓	✓	✓	✓
Age in years						✓	✓	✓	✓	✓
Relationship to head of household						✓	✓	✓	✓	✓
Marital status						✓	✓	✓	✓	✓
Place of birth					✓	✓	✓	✓	✓	✓
Occupation*	✓	✓	✓	✓	✓	✓	✓	✓	✓	✓
School attendance							✓	✓	✓	
Infirmity (deaf, dumb, blind, lunatic,etc)						✓	✓	✓	✓	✓

49

today, and they gradually became more accurate. The introduction of civil registration for births, marriages and deaths in 1837 led to increased knowledge about the growth of the population and its state of health. In 1841, the Registrar took over responsibility for the census from parish officials, and the names and occupations of people living in each household were now given for the first time. The 1851 census added questions about age, marital status and relationship to the head of the household. The basic pattern for future censuses had now been set.

From 1841, census returns were drawn up by Enumerators who wrote the information onto printed sheets, household by household. Each household had a schedule number by which it could be identified. Details were taken of everyone staying in the house on the night of the census. The page (figure 41) from the Enumerator's Returns for Liverpool in 1851 shows how the information was set out. Even a small example can provide interesting insights into the size and make-up of families, the extent of their mobility and the nature of their occupations.

Once names and addresses were included on census forms, questions of confidentiality arose and it became necessary to reassure those who gave the information that it would not be revealed to anyone else. A rule was made, and is still in operation, that Enumerators' Returns would not be made public for a hundred years. This means that they are now available for the censuses from 1841 to 1881 (censuses before 1841 only produced statistical summaries).

No such secrecy restricted the publication of basic population figures, and printed reports were published in book form after each census. This makes it possible to trace the pattern of population growth in local communities from 1801 to the present day. The printed reports give population tables for each parish, and information about ages, occupations, places of birth and public health is summarised for each part of the country. The page from the printed report of the 1851 census (figure 42) gives the number of houses and the number of people in parishes in Bradford and Halifax from

▲
41   Enumerators' Returns for Liverpool, 1851.

1801 up to 1851. The figures make the growth rate over these fifty years dramatically clear.

Where to Find Census Records

Printed census reports summarising the population statistics from each census are available in bound volumes in Record Offices and larger libraries. Enumerators' Returns for the censuses from 1841 to 1881 have now been made public. Copies have been made in most areas of the country, mainly on microfilm, but sometimes in the form of photocopied books. They can usually be found in the Record Office or the main library. The original returns are held at the Public Record Office, Chancery Lane, London and photocopies of specific pages can be supplied on request.

Questions Census Records Can Help to Answer

How large was the population of a particular place? (Printed reports)

Can the various occupants of a particular house be traced? (Enumerators' Returns)

How large were families or households? (Printed reports of Enumerators' Returns)

What proportion of people were still living in their place of birth? (Enumerators' Returns)

What were the occupations of the people living in a particular area? (Enumerators' Returns)

What was the rate of population growth over a given period? (Printed reports)

42 ▼ Part of a page from the printed report of the 1851 Census, showing figures for Halifax and Bradford.

13
Directories

Directories were local handbooks with a commercial purpose. They gave factual information about towns and villages, and listed residents and tradesmen. Some directories were being produced by the end of the eighteenth century, but most date from the mid-nineteenth century onwards.

Dozens of different directories were published and a selection can now be found on the shelves of Record Offices and libraries. The most widely available are Kelly's Directories (which started off as Post Office Directories until Mr Kelly left the Post Office to set up his own directory publishing company in the 1870s). Kelly's Directories proved very successful and most other directories follow a fairly similar format.

To begin with, directories usually covered a large group of counties, but they were later

43 Entry for Beckley in the Sussex Post Office Directory, 1878.

▼

BECKLEY is a parish in the Eastern division of the county, hundred of Goldspur, union and county court district of Rye, rape of Hastings, rural deanery of Icklesham, archdeaconry of Lewes, and diocese of Chichester, 6½ miles west-north-west from Rye. The river Rother bounds this parish on the north, separating Sussex from Kent. The church of All Saints consists of chancel, nave and aisles, with a small tower and spire containing 6 bells. The register dates from the year 1597. The living is a rectory, yearly value £850, with residence, in the gift of the Master and Fellows of University College, Oxford, and held by the Rev. Thomas Shadforth, M.A. formerly fellow of that college. Here is a place of worship for Wesleyan Methodists. Thomas Smith-Pix, esq. J.P. is lord of the manor. The principal landowners are Thomas Frewen, Edward Pennyfather, and Frank Smith, esqs. The soil is loamy ; subsoil, clay. The chief crops are wheat and hops. The area is 5,316 acres ; rateable value, £6,686 10s.; and the population in 1871 was 1,367.

Parish Clerk, Henry Larkin.

Post & Money Order Office & Savings Bank.— William Maynard, receiver. Letters arrive from Ashford at 5.45 a.m. & 12.30 p.m.; dispatched at 3 & 10.15 p.m.; on sundays 5.45 ; dispatched at 10.15

Police Station, William Elphick, sergeant, & 5 men
National School, John O'Connell, master
Carriers.—*See* Northiam

Bishop Mrs
Collins Edward Lorton
Ginn Mrs
Perry Richard, Chestnut lodge
Shadforth Rev. Thomas, M.A. [rector]
Smith Mrs. Woodgate
Stonham Godfrey
Woodham John

COMMERCIAL.

Ashenden James, farmer
Ballard Ebenezer, farmer, Oak hill
Beaney William, wheelwright
Bexhill Frances (Mrs.), *Rose & Crown*
Bishop Mrs. & Miss, ladies' school

Brown William, farmer
Butler Thomas, grocer
Caffyn Joseph, miller
Cole John, shoemaker
Collins Edward Lorton, surgeon
Cooper Charles, farmer
Davis Robert, chimney sweeper
Dunk Robert, saddler
Hammond Charles, cooper
Harvey Stephen, timber merchant
Maynard Jemima (Mrs.). *Royal Oak*
Maynard William, grocer, draper & post office
Ranger Spencer, beer retailer
Reeve William, farmer, Gate farm

Roberts Albert, farmer
Russell Alfred, farmer
Russell Isaac, carpenter
Russell John, farmer
Russell Thomas, grocer
Russell Walter, butcher
Selmes James, farmer, Methersham
Skinner John, wheelwright
Smith Alfred, painter & house decorator
Smith Tilden, farmer
Springett George, tailor
Stonham Godfrey, farmer
Vincent James, butcher
Weston John, grocer & draper
Willsher Thomas, farmer, Hayes

produced for one county at a time, with extensive coverage of the major towns. Kelly's Directories for most counties were published at about five- or seven-year intervals from the mid-nineteenth century until 1940. Since that date, they have only been produced for large provincial towns.

Directories open up a goldmine of local information. Large towns receive lengthy coverage, but even the smallest village is fully described. The entry for Beckley in Sussex (figure 43), which appeared in the Post Office Directory for 1878, is fairly typical. Details about the village's situation and place in the local administrative system are included and information is given about the local institutions of church and chapel, Post Office, Police Station and National School. The soil and the crops grown in the area are described, and the main landowners are named, along with other important residents. The list of "commercial" residents shows the self-sufficiency of a small community, and makes for interesting comparison with the present day. Entries such as this provide valuable background information which can be used for building up a picture of a community at a particular time, or for tracing how it changed and developed over a longer period.

44 Street directory for Cardiff in Kelly's Directory of Monmouthshire and South Wales, 1895.

ALBERT STREET—continued.
PILLAR LETTER BOX
56 Floyd Mrs. Jane, dress ma

Alexander road, Canton, 305 Cowbridge road.
WEST SIDE.
2 Hill Henry, art master
6 Norman Robert John,clerk
8 NormanHy. master marinr
12 Miller John, coal dealer
16 ThomasMrs.Maria,aptmts
24 Watkins Chas.chief enginr
26 HoltWm.Walt.chief engnr
28 Codd Thomas, plasterer
30 Wills James, gilder
40 Clark Geo.market gardenr
56 AtkinsonSydney,mfrs'.agt
80 Davies Charles, shopkeepr
.....here is Commercial st......
South Wales Jam & Marmalade Co. Limited (John Hudson, managing directr)
EAST SIDE.
21 Edwards Mrs
29 Evans William Henry, teacher of music
.... here is Eton pl ....
33 Williams Mrs
45 Bussell Edwd.shipping agt

Alexander street, Cathays, Woodville road.
Geen William, builder
138 Cardiff Shoe Black Brigade Depôt (William George Cadby, managr)

Alfred street, Roath, 83 Albany road to Ninian road.
WEST SIDE.

Andrew's buildings.
See PENARTH ROAD.

Angelina street, Bute st. Maria st. to Loudoun square.
3 Dixon John, boarding ho
8 Childs Henry, seamen's boarding house
12 Marsh William, butcher
13 PedwellSaml.Edwd.shpkpr
........here is Sophia st.........
Marchioness of Bute inn, Henry Barber
21 Cogholo Francesco, shpkpr
23 Kerman Mrs. Elizh.grocer
...... here is Loudoun sq ......
Westgate inn, Thos. Williams
... here are Francis st. Sophia st. & Nelson st......
Bute Castle P.H. Rd. Williams

Anglesey street, Canton, 17 Pen-y-peel rd.toRadnor rd.
4 Griffiths David, milk dealr
11 Loud Mrs. Fanny,shopkpr

Angus street, Roath, 99 Albany road to Dalcross st.
WEST SIDE.
69 Burns Daniel
Carter Arthur Francis
EAST SIDE.
2 Chaplin Mrs. Emily, pork butcher
4 Smith Albert, shoe maker
6 Candy Mrs. Clara,milliner
24 David Phillip
24 Dillon Herbert Edgar
36 Watts Miss Mary, stocking knitter

62 Clapp George
64 Knapman William
66 Bucknell William Fredk
68 Boughton Robert James
70 Stokes Arthur
72 Jeffrys William
74 Rogers Alfd. marine engnr
86 Taylor George
88 Jackson Charles Haddon
124 Woodruff Miss Anna, dress maker
140 Bennet Samuel
160 DallimoreWalt.Rd.grocer

Arthur street, Roath, 170 Broadway to Pearl street.
33 Hamlin Mrs.Mary, shpkpr
10 Evans Albert, milk dealer

Atlas chambers.
See JAMES STREET.

Atlas road, Canton, continuation of Wellington street to Commercial st.
Kyte George & Co. engineers (Atlas works)

Atlas terrace.
Now called ATLAS ROAD.

Augusta street,Splotlands, Moira place to Meteor st.
1 Brooks William, shopkpr
22 Herd Fredk. tea dealer
28 Fry Charles, grocer
........here is Meteor st.........
29 Taylor Henry Harrison, general draper
38 Coakley Cornelius, shpkpr

EAST SIDE.
2 Roath Park Coal Co. coal mers. & furn. removers
2 Geach Frederick Charles
4 Geach Ernest
6 Francis Henry Robert
8 Phillips David
10 Tonkin John Charles
14 Davies Mrs.Charlte.Nalder
16 Wallis Simon Thomas
18 Needle William
24 Sargeaunt John Bird
26 Rule Hy. master mariner
28 Leng Rd. master mariner
30 Culley David
34 Frost Edward

Bank buildings.
See ST. MARY STREET.

Barley Mow lane, Canton, North Morgan st. to Ann st.
Hill J. G. & Co. cabinet mas
Deacon Alfred, timber mer

Beda road, Canton, 349 Cowbridge road.
3 Chell Francis
5 Angier Walter, com. agent
7 Johnson Wm. markt.grdnr
9 Newberry Chas. W. clerk
11 McIntyre Robt. journalist
2 Roberts Mrs

Beauchamp st. Canton, 46 Tudor st. to Despenser st.
EAST SIDE.
4 HastrickHy.Thos.engineer
6 Birtwistle William Robert
8 Cording John

BRADFORD'S
PATENT WASHING MACHINERY.

**BRADFORD'S PATENT
"ACORN" INDIA RUBBER
CLOTHES WRINGER.**
See Catalogue, page 24.

**BRADFORD'S IMPROVED "PREMIER"
BOX MANGLE.**—*See Catalogue, page* 29.

LONDON, 1862.

"We have never had any Washing Machine that has
given such complete satisfaction to every class of
purchaser and user."

THOMAS BRADFORD & CO., Patentees.

DUBLIN, 1865.

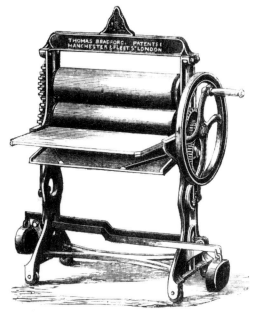

**BRADFORD'S PATENT WRINGING
AND MANGLING MACHINE.**
See Catalogue, page 23.

**BRADFORD'S NEW PATENT "VOWEL"
WASHING, WRINGING AND MANGLING
MACHINE.**—*See Catalogue, page* 10.

GENERAL ILLUSTRATED CATALOGUE OF WASHING MACHINERY, LAUNDRY FITTINGS FOR HOTELS, SCHOOLS, HOSPITALS,
WORKHOUSES, &c., 64 PAGES, FREE BY POST ON APPLICATION.

THOS. BRADFORD & CO., { 63, Fleet Street, LONDON.
Cathedral Steps, MANCHESTER.
23, Dawson Street, DUBLIN.

The entries for towns provide even more information, listing council members and magistrates, schools, hospitals, churches and local societies. The means of transport (railway, omnibus, etc) are described and details are given about post and carrier services and local newspapers. Rather like the "yellow pages" of telephone books today, directories attempted to give comprehensive information about trades and services. In towns, all tradesmen were listed with their addresses, either alphabetically by name, or under their respective occupations (Chair Makers, Chandlers, Charcoal Burners, Cheese Factors, etc).

From the end of the nineteenth century, street directories were usually included, arranged as shown in figure 44. The streets are listed alphabetically, and house numbers are given, with the names and trades of the occupants. These street directories are useful for reconstructing the pattern of trade and industry in a particular area, and for plotting how it changed over the years. They are also invaluable for tracing the history of a particular street or house.

A large part of each directory was made up of advertisements. These included "county advertisements" from local manufacturers, and a section of "London advertisements". Advertisements explaining the merits of agricultural implements, building materials, boilers and pumps were included alongside advertisements singing the praises of schools for young ladies and the latest styles of clothing. The Victorian drive for improvement in all areas of life is reflected in advertisements for water closets, baths and heating systems and for cures and remedies with amazing powers. The advertisement for Bradford's washing machinery (figure 45) shows a typical confidence in the virtues of the products being illustrated.

Where to Find Directories

Record Offices and libraries usually have good collections of directories on their reference shelves. The range of directories and the dates for which they are available vary from county to county, but most counties were well-covered from the 1860s onwards.

Questions Directories Can Help to Answer

Can the development of a particular street be traced over a period of time?

How does the range of occupations compare with the present day?

Can the building of churches, chapels, schools, hospitals, etc, be dated?

What do the advertisements show about contemporary life?

What services did the community provide? (carrier, post, public transport, education, etc?)

Who were considered the "important" residents in the area?

◀ 45   Advertisement from the "London" section in the Sussex Post Office Directory, 1867.

14
Local Newspapers

From the eighteenth century onwards the whole complexity and variety of everyday life can be found recorded in local newspapers. The wealth of information provided can be overwhelming. There is rarely an index listing references to a particular topic, but local or national events for which the dates are known can be tracked down fairly easily. At a more general level, a single copy of a local newspaper can be used to gain an inside view of contemporary concerns.

The first provincial newspapers were produced in the early eighteenth century. They often had a wide circulation and, to begin with, national and international news dominated over local events. During the nineteenth century, weekly or daily newspapers sprang up in even the smallest of towns, and the reporting became more local in character.

At first sight, eighteenth- and nineteenth-century newspapers may seem very dull to the modern reader. The print is tiny and densely packed into long columns. Headlines are small and hardly break up the mass of print. Even in the early twentieth century it can be unusual to find a picture or a photograph, and advertisers' drawings can be a welcome relief!

The original readers were used to extracting their information about the outside world from the printed word, and local newspapers reflect this thirst for detail. Railway timetables are given in full, corn prices and population statistics are meticulously recorded, and public meetings, court proceedings and funerals are reported down to the last detail.

Yet, behind the dullness of the print, there is plenty of emotion and excitement. There are dramatic and highly-coloured descriptions of crimes and hangings, fires, disasters and strange happenings. There is plenty of indignant debate about local change and development, and the advertisements offer to put all wrongs to right, with solutions for every problem.

The front page of the *Northampton Mercury* for 24 April 1790, part of which is shown in figure 46, illustrates the spread of coverage provided by a local newspaper. A parliamentary candidate states his case. Notice is given of moves to repair the gaol and build a new House of Correction. The fees to be taken by Clerks to the Justices are listed. Notice is given of a meeting of Turnpike Trustees, and of properties to be let. London news recounts what has been going on in Parliament, and spicy and dramatic snippets from around the country are included.

Local newspapers can help put human flesh on the skeleton of information provided by other records, showing that developments in local life were widely discussed and were of real concern to ordinary people.

Where to Find Local Newspapers

Local newspaper offices usually hold complete sets of back-numbers, which can be seen by appointment.

Many Record Offices and libraries hold good collections of old newspapers, either in bound volumes, or on microfilm. Newspaper articles about a particular topic are sometimes listed in the general subject index in the Record Office.

Questions Local Newspapers Can Help to Answer

How did national events affect the local community?

What was the response to local developments (e.g. the coming of the railway, or gas-lighting?)

What were the main concerns of a community at a particular date?

What do the advertisements indicate about people's needs?

46 *The Northampton Mercury*, 24 April 1790.

▼

. LXXI. THE No 7.

NORTHAMPTON MERCURY.

dy Money with Advertisements.] SATURDAY, APRIL 24, 1790. [Price Threepence Halfpenny.]

This PAPER, for upwards of Seventy Years past, has been, and continues to be, circulated in all the Market-Towns and populous Villages in the Counties of *Northampton, Leicester, Nottingham, Lincoln, Rutland, Huntingdon, Cambridge*, and Isle of *Ely, Essex, Bedford, Hertford, Buckingham, Berks, Oxford, Warwick* to *Birmingham*, and *Stafford, &c.* and by the Post to greater Distances.——It is also regularly sent to the *Chapter, London*, and *Peele's* Coffee-Houses, *London*.

☞ Persons who live at a Distance from Places the Newsmen pass through, may have this Paper sent by Post (free of Expence) or left at any convenient Place they shall appoint, by sending their Orders to the Printers.

unday and Tuesday's Posts.

LONDON, *April* 20.

LAST Saturday's Gazette contains two Proclamations by the Lord - Lieutenant of Ireland; one for dissolving the Parliament of that Kingdom, and the other for calling a new one on the 20th of May.

In the House of Commons on Friday, Mr. Sheridan made his promised on, for a Repeal of the Bill passed last Session, sting the Manufacture of Tobacco to the Survey e Excise. At Half past Three o'Clock on Satur- Morning the House divided, when there appeared ne Motion 147, against it 191; Majority 44.

e Industry used to procure a full House was the as employed in the Case of the Dissenters—but ecision was in every Respect different. The To- Manufacturers, in our Opinion, have no little to rejoice. A Majority of only 44 on the Side dministration, when the House contains (besides who are paired of) 338 Members, is surely no ry, and Sir Robert Walpole gave up this very , although his Majority was upwards of *sixty*. best Friends of Administration must allow that s the most troublesome Business they have had to unter.

e public Revenue has had an unexpected Increase Week of 7160l. sent to the Commissioners of e by an unknown Hand; of which they have public Notice.

turday the Lord-Chancellor committed the Rev. Stevens to the Fleet Prison, for carrying a young of the Name of Jefferies to Gretna-Green, where as married to her, she being a Ward of the Court hancery.—The Mother, Aunt, and other Rela-, and Friends of the Lady, all bore honourable mony by their Affidavits to the Character of Mr. ens, and deposed that they approved of the riage, although it was contracted without their ty.—The Lord-Chancellor said there could be no se for a *Clergyman* of the established Church ing a Ward of the Court to Scotland, and there married by a *Blacksmith*. The Protection of the ds of that Court was of great Importance. His ship, however, paid due Attention to the Affi- s, which he said might become a Subject of future ideration.

. Murray, who some Weeks since descended from mouth Church-Tower in a Parachute, on Wed- ay came down from the Bell Tower of Chichester edral, but not with the same Success. When t 14 Feet from the Top, a sudden Gust of Wind this bold aerostatic Adventurer and the Apparatus horizontal Position: When on a Level with the er of the Cathedral he righted, but an eddy d threw him a second Time horizontally, in which ation he fell to the Ground with great Force. The d gushed from his Ears, Nose, and Mouth, most ifully; and he was carried to the Blue-Anchor

walking more than a hundred Yards before them, when he heard the Deceased cry aloud, "Antonio—O Antonio!" that he ran back, and found him lifeless, with one Arm broken and his Skull fractured, which he learnt was done by Apologi in knocking him down, and that his Throat was cut in two Places by Farari, with a Knife which he had borrowed of him that Morning. That he was in great Horror at the Sight of such a Spectacle; but assisted in burying the Body, for Fear of a Discovery, and that he should be deemed an Accessary in the Murder. Apologi and Farari acknowledged all he thus said was strictly true. On ascending the Scaffold, Apologi and Farari discovered great Perturbation of Mind, and wept abundantly. Marini deported himself with more Fortitude, and yet with becoming Decency.—Thomas Hewitt Masters likewise shewed a becoming Contrition. After a few Minutes spent in Devotion with their respective Ministers, the Drop fell. After hanging the usual Time, their Bodies were cut down, and sent to Surgeons'-Hall for Dissection.

COUNTRY NEWS.

SHREWSBURY, *April* 16. Wednesday Night last a dreadful Fire broke out at a Farm near Whitchurch, which destroyed all the Out Buildings; 25 Cows and 14 Horses were burnt, with a Quantity of Corn, Hay, &c. The Loss is very great.

STAMFORD, *April* 16. On Wednesday Se'nnight, at the Wheat-Sheaf, at Werrington, near Peterborough, an English Cannibal of the Name of Joshua Thorp, undertook to eat Half a Pound of Candles, and drink two Quarts of Ale at two immediately repeated Draughts, which he performed with great Ease in seven Minutes, and then challenged the Company to give him a similar Quantity; but the Proposal was denied.

To the Worthy and Independent ELECTORS *of the Town of* NORTHAMPTON.

GENTLEMEN,

MR. TROTMAN *having publicly signified his Intention of not offering himself a Candidate for the Town of Northampton at the ensuing General Election, I embrace so good an Opportunity of offering my Services to you, and of soliciting the Favour of your Votes and Interest to succeed him.*

Permit me to assure you, that if I should be so fortunate as to have the Honour of being elected, it shall be my Study steadily to pursue that Conduct which may gain me your Approbation; and by an uniform Attention to your Interest, shew my Sense of the Obligation conferred on me.

As soon as Parliament is dissolved, I shall take the earliest Opportunity of waiting on you in Person.

I have the Honour to be,

GENTLEMEN,

Your most obedient,

And faithful, humble Servant,

E. BOUVERIE.

RUGBY ANNIVERSARY.

NORTHAMPTONSHIRE.

PURSUANT to the Directions of the Act of Parliament made in the 24th Year of His present Majesty's Reign, for explaining and amending an Act made in the 11th and 12th Years of the Reign of King William the Third, intituled, "An Act to enable Justices of Peace to build and repair Gaols in their respective Counties," and for other Purposes therein mentioned; His Majesty's Justices of the Peace in and for the County of Northampton, assembled at their General Quarter-Sessions of the Peace holden at Northampton, in and for the said County, on Thursday in the first Week next after the Close of Easter; to wit, the 15th Day of April, in the 30th Year of the Reign of His Majesty King George the Third, and in the Year of our Lord 1790, do give Notice, that the Grand Jury at the last Lent Assizes held in and for the said County, did present the Gaol of and for the said County of Northampton, situate and being in the Town of Northampton, in the said County, to be insufficient and inconvenient, for Want of rebuilding and enlarging the same, and by Reason thereof to be too small, close and confined, and wholly insufficient and unsafe for the due and safe Keeping and Confinement, separating and securing of the Felons, Debtors, and other Prisoners committed to the said Gaol; and that they, the said Justices, will take the said Presentment into Consideration at the next ensuing General Quarter-Sessions of the Peace to be holden in and for the said County of Northampton. By Order of the Court,

CHR. SMYTH, Clerk of the Peace.

NORTHAMPTONSHIRE.

NOTICE is hereby given, That His Majesty's Justices of the Peace for the County of Northampton, assembled in their Quarter-Sessions held at Northampton, on the 15th Day of April, 1790, have resolved to borrow and take up at Interest, on Mortgage of the County Rates, at the next General Quarter-Sessions of the Peace to be holden for the said County on Thursday the 15th Day of July next, the Sum of TWO THOUSAND POUNDS, in Sums not less than 50l. nor exceeding 100l. each, towards defraying the Expences of BUILDING a NEW HOUSE of CORRECTION at the Town of NORTHAMPTON, for the said County of Northampton, pursuant to the Power given to them for that Purpose in and by the Act of Parliament of the 24th Year of His present Majesty's Reign, for explaining and amending an Act made in the 22d Year of the Reign of His present Majesty, intitled an Act for the amending and rendering more effectual the Laws in being relative to Houses of Correction.—Such Persons, therefore, who are willing to lend Money on the above-mentioned Security, are desired to signify to the Clerk of the Peace what Sums they will advance, and at what Rate of Interest.

The Interest will be regularly paid Half-yearly, as it becomes due; and when the Justices shall think fit to pay off any Part of the Principal Money, due Notice will be given thereof, and it will be determined by Ballot in what Order the several Securities are to be discharged.

CHR. SMYTH, Clerk of the Peace.

NORTHAMPTON, 15th April, 1790.

A TABLE of the FEES

To be taken by the CLERKS to the JUSTICES of the PEACE within the County of NORTHAMPTON,

Instead of the Fees contained in any former Table, made, settled and approved in the Year 1789, and ratified and confirmed by Mr. Baron THOMSON, at the Lent Assize, 1790.

	l.	s.	d.
FOR every Information, Examination, Summons except in Behalf of a Pauper, Warrant except in Felony, Order except respecting Vagrants, Judgment or Conviction except on penal Statutes, where one Justice only is necessary, — — —	0	1	0
For the same (except as aforesaid) where two Justices are necessary, to each Clerk 1s.—Total —	0	2	0
For every Summons in Behalf of a Pauper, and for			

OSWESTRY FAIR.

THE FAIR for the Town of OSWESTRY, in the County of Salop, which for some Years last past, hath been held on the 1st Day of May, will this present Year, and altogether in future, be held on the 12th Day of May yearly, being the Day on which by the Charter of the said Town, and by ancient Custom, the said Fair is, and ought to be held.

JOHN GIBBONS, Mayor.
W. M. OWEN, High Steward.
LEWIS JONES, Coroner.

OSWESTRY, 7th April, 1790.

TO be LETT, and Entered on immediately, or at Midsummer next,

That well-known INN, the BEAR, in SHEEP-STREET, NORTHAMPTON, now in the Occupation of Mr. Thomas Powell, who is going to retire from the Public Business.

Likewise to be Sold, the Household Goods, Brewing-Utensils, Stock of Ale and Liquors, at a fair Appraisement.

For Particulars, enquire of Mr. Cole, Attorney, Northampton.

APRIL 3, 1790.

TO be SOLD, A WOOD, situate in the Lordship of MAIDWELL, in the County of Northampton, known by the Name of SCOTLAND-WOOD, and containing 62 Acres, or thereabouts. There is a considerable Quantity of fine thriving Oak, Ash, Elm, Poplar and Fir Timber therein, besides Underwood.

Enquire of Messrs. Smyth and Butcher, Attornies, Northampton.

To TANNERS.

TO be LETT, either on Lease, or otherwise, and Entered upon immediately, at ROWELL, in the County of Northampton,

A Capital MESSUAGE or DWELLING-HOUSE, with the Tan-Yards, Vats, Kiln, Mill, Barns, Storehouses, Drying-Houses, Stables, Gardens, and every other Convenience for the Business of a Tanner.

The Premises are well situated for Markets, Bark, Hydes, &c. and calculated for carrying on an extensive Business in the Tanning Line; for which Purpose they have been used upwards of fifty Years.

For Particulars, and Terms, apply to Mr. Samuel Cave, of Rowell; or Roberts and Marshall, Kettering.

NOTICE is hereby given, That a Meeting of the Trustees appointed by Act of Parliament for repairing the Road from the Dun-Cow in the Town of Dunchurch, in the County of Warwick, to St. James's End, in the Parish of Duston, in the County of Northampton, will be held at the House of Mr. Walton, known by the Sign of the Fox-and-Hounds, at Harlestone, in the said County of Northampton, on Monday the 10th Day of May next, at Eleven o'Clock in the Forenoon of the same Day, for electing new Trustees of the said Road in the Room of such Trustees who are dead.——And at which Meeting the TOLLS arising at the several Gates upon the said Turnpike-Road, called or known by the several Names of HILLMORTON GATE, WEST-HADDON GATE, and DUSTON GATE, will be LETT by AUCTION, to the BEST BIDDERS, between the Hours of Twelve and Two o'Clock, in the Manner directed by the Act passed in the 13th Year of His present Majesty's Reign, "For Regulating the Turnpike-Roads;" which several Tolls produced the last Year the respective Sums following (viz.) at Hillmorton Gate the Sum of 84l.; West-Haddon Gate the Sum of 156l.; and Duston Gate the Sum of 125l.; above the Expences of collecting them, and will be put up at those respective Sums. Whoever happen to be the best Bidders, must, at the same Time, give Security, with sufficient Sureties, to the Satisfaction of the Trustees of the said Turnpike-Road, for Payment of the respective Rents agreed for, and at such respective Times as they shall direct.

By Order of the Trustees.

NORTHAMPTON, April 3d, 1790. CHR. SMYTH.

15
Personal Documents

Many large landowning families have accumulated family records over generations and even centuries. Such collections of family archives have now, in many cases, been deposited in Record Offices.

Estate and family papers of this kind usually include documents concerning the running of the house and the administration of the surrounding estates; title deeds, wills and inventories, business correspondence and accounts. The family's role in the community may also be reflected in documents concerning military, judicial or political affairs, or the organization of charities. Finally, there may be a wealth of rather more personal family correspondence, giving accounts of foreign tours or journeys to different parts of the country, or describing, often in amusing detail, the people met, the meals eaten and the places visited in the course of everyday life. Such letters vary from the beautifully legible, to rapidly scrawled missives in faded ink on wafer-thin paper, sent through the post in large quantities during Victorian times.

As well as these large collections, personal documents of various kinds have come to light at various times behind fireplaces, under thatched roofs or simply in attics. Letters and diaries, bills and accounts, indentures and wills can all help to re-create the life and times of the people they belonged to, and reveal something about their personalities.

Diaries are particularly fascinating. Some are little more than note-books containing jottings about business affairs. Others give a far more vivid insight into the thoughts and feelings of the writer. John Clifton of Oundle kept a diary for fifteen years, at the end of the eighteenth century. In these diaries or "day books", he gives an account of his work as a joiner. He also records local scandal and gossip with great relish, and comments sceptically on newspaper reports about flying "aerostatic machines" and the finding of twelve-foot long human skeletons. In the extracts in figure 47, he records some of the outrageous events which added spice to ordinary life.

It should never be forgotten that today soon becomes tomorrow's history, and the letters and diaries, scrapbooks and photographs which many families have inherited from previous generations can all help to re-create a vanished past.

Where to Find Personal Records

Many family and estate papers have been deposited in Record Offices. They are catalogued under the family name, or sometimes under the place of residence. There is usually a full list of the documents included in the collection. Diaries may be found under the writer's name, or listed in the "diaries" section of a subject catalogue.

Letters are usually catalogued under the name of an individual and large numbers appear in family collections. Letters about a particular topic may be listed in the subject index, and correspondence concerning local improvements, etc, can often be found amongst Quarter Sessions and council papers. Individuals within the community own personal records of all kinds which can throw light on events in the not-too-distant past.

Questions Personal Records Can Help to Answer

What do the letters and/or diary of an individual show about his life and character?

What do letters and diaries reveal about life in the local community?

To what extent are national events reflected in personal records?

What help can old family photographs, scrapbooks, etc, be in reconstructing a picture of life at a particular time?

What was involved in the running of a large estate?

47 The Diary of John Clifton of Oundle, Northamptonshire, 1779. (Transcript on page 65)

▼

Transcripts

Transcripts of fifteen of the more difficult-to-read documents are included here. The original spelling has been kept, but abbreviated words have been written in full, in order to make the meaning clearer.

Glebe Terrier of the Church's Property at Broadway, 1715 (fig. 12)

	A Terrier of All the Houses and Lands and Proffitts belonging to the Viccarage of Broadway made the fourteenth day of June One Thousand Seven Hundred and ffifteene
Imprimis	One dwelling House with a Garden and Backside thereunto belonging
Item	Three Leyes lying at the South End of the said Backside and called by the Name of the Crofts.
Item	One Acre of arable Land or thereabouts lying within a Meadow called Squabb and knowne by the name of the Viccarage Acre.
Item	The Churchyard of the said Parish Church.
Item	One Moiety of the Tithe Lambs Issuing and falling upon One Hundred and Twelve Yard Lands in Broadway aforesaid
Item	Three Quarters of a Yard Land lying dispersed in the Comon ffeild of Broadway aforesaid knowne by the name of Sheldon's Three Quarters Land with two Cow Pastures and the Usuall Sheep pastures thereunto belonging.
Item	One Peice of Arable Land conteyning Sixteene Acres And alsoe Another peice of Arable Land adjoyning conteyning Seaventeen Acres or thereabouts both lying in the parish of Mickleton in the County of Gloucester and knowne by the Names of Upper Butterhill and Longlands.
Item	Two other peices of arable or pasture ground Conteyning Twenty Acres or thereabouts lying in the said parish of Mickleton and knowne by the names of Lower Butterhill and Washpool Leyes.
Item	One Peice of Meadowground adjoyning to the said Lower Butterhill Conteyning ffive Acres or thereabouts.

Jane Wallet's Apprenticeship Indenture, 1727 (fig. 23)

This Indenture Witnesseth That Jane Wallet pauper being fatherless and Motherless and / Wholly provided for by ye parish officers of Cowbit in the County of Lincoln Doth by the advice and Assistance of / John Brainsby Churchwarden and John Cock and Henry Stevenson Overseers of the poor of the said parish put / and place herself Apprentice to John Hood of Moulton in the said County of Lincoln farmer with him to / dwell and Serve from the date of these presents untill she shall Accomplish her full Age of One and / Twenty years during which Terme the said Apprentice her said Master faithfully shall Serve in all / Lawfull business According to her power Wit and Ability and honestly Orderly and Obediently in all / things demean and behave herself towards her said Master and all his during the said terme And the said / John Hood for himself his Executors Administrators and Assignes (in consideracon of the Sum of Five pounds of / of lawful money of Great Brittain to him in hand paid by the parishioners of Cowbitt aforesaid the / Receipt whereof he doth hereby Acknowledge) doth Covenant and grant to and with you the said Churchwardens and / overseers and Every of them and their Successors for the Time being by these presents That he or they the said / Apprentice in the Art of Houswifry shall and will teach and instruct and also shall and will during the said / Terme find provide and allow unto the said Apprentice meet Competent and Sufficient Meat Drink and Apparel / Lodging Washing and all other things Necessary and fitt for an Apprentice And also shall and will so / provide for the said Apprentice that she be not any Way a Charge to the said parish or parishioners of Cowbitt / but of and from all Charge shall and will save ye said parish and parishioners harmless and / indemnified during the said Term

And at the end of the said Term shall and will make provide allow and / deliver unto the said Apprentice double Apparel of all sorts good and New (that is to say) a good new Suit / for the Holy days and another for the Working Days In Witness whereof the parties aforesaid have / to these present Indentures Interchangably put their hands and Seals this fourteenth day of March Anno Domini 1726/7

                    John Hood

Sealed and Delivered (being legally Stampt)

Surveyor of the Highways Accounts, 1793 (fig. 15)

The Disburstments of John Wigginton Surveyor of the Highways from Michaelmas 1792 to Ditto 1793	£	s	d
1793			
May 29 — Paid at Barnoak, Ale for Teams	—	6	6
June 2nd — Paid Jonathen Hudson, 2 Days Work	—	2	8
Ditto 9 — Paid George Bains, 8 Days Ditto	—	9	4
Ditto 16 — To 2 Floors of Gravel taking up	—	6	—
Ditto — Paid George Bains 6 Days Works	—	7	—
Ditto 23 — Paid Ditto . . . 3 Days Ditto	—	3	6
To these Accounts making out	—	1	—
Ditto — To 14 Loads of Gravel	—	7	—
Ditto 30 — Paid George Bains 4 Days Work	—	4	8
July 21 — Paid Mrs. Gray, Ale for Labourers	—	5	6
Paid Thomas Read for Bread	—	—	2
Paid Mrs. Blake, 3 Quarts of Ale, at 2 Tunnels	—	1	—
Paid Bennet Sarjant, as by Bill	—	2	—
Paid Robert Bothway, as by Bill	—	8	6
Paid for Stone, as by Bill	1	10	11
Paid for the Abstract	—	3	—
A Journey to Peterborough	—	1	6
Disbursted	£5	—	4

Sarah Abearne's Will, 1703 (fig. 34)

In the Name of God Amen I Sarah Abearne of Irchester in the County of Northampton Widow being of sound and perfect Disposing mind memory and understanding doe make and ordaine this my last will and Testament in manner and form ffollowing viz: Imprimis I bequeth my soul into ye hands of Almighty God my Creator Trusting to be saved by the Alone meritts of my Lord and Saviour Jesus Christ my Body to be decently buried att the discretion of my Executrix hereafter named, as for my Temporall Estate my mind is they should be disposed off as follows, First I Doe and bequeth unto son Will Abearn of Kimbolton in the County of Huntington Tanner one shilling All the rest of my Goods chattells, with Rent or arrears of Rent and All other my personall estate whatsoever I doe Give and bequeth to my Daughter Bridgitt Abearne of Irchester in ye said County of northampton whom I doe make sole Executrix of This my last will and Testament and I doe hereby revoke all former wills by me heretofore made I witness wherof I the above named Sarah Abearne have herunto sett my hand and seal this fourteenth day of ffebruary in the second year of ye Raign of our soveraign Lady Ann by the Grace of God of England Scotland France and Ireland Queen defender of the ffaith Anno Domini

                    1703

Calendar of Prisoners in the Newport House of Correction, 1789 (fig. 19)

Essex	(Newport House of Correction Kallender, to and for (the Christmas quarter Sessions January 1789
Conveyed on the 11th November 1788, and Publickly whipped in the Town of Waltham Holy Cross, and then discharged	(John Newman, Convicted of Grand Larceny, at the last (Michaelmas quarter Sessions October 8th 1788, was ordered to be (kept to hard Labour until the 11th of November following, at (which time he was ordered to be Conveyed to Waltham (Holy Cross, and there publickly whipped from the New (Inn to the Church, Between the Hours of 12 and one (oClock, and then Discharged
Time Expired and was Discharged the 18th November 1788	(Peter Carroll Convicted of a Misdemeanor at the last (Michaelmas quarter Session October 8th 1788, to be kept to hard (Labour for Six Weeks, and then to be Discharged
Discharged 9th November 1788 having Sattisfied the penalty	(George Moule of Saffron Walden Committed 6th November 1788, by William (Gretton Clerk, to be Safely kept for three Months, being Convicted (upon the oath of John Chapman a Credible Witness, for that he (the said George Moule, Not being a person by the Laws of this (Realm quallified so to do, on the 11th February at Saffron Walden (aforesaid Did keep and use an Engine for the Destruction of the (Game Called a Snare, whereof he forfieted the Sum of five (pounds, and whereas it duly appears upon the oath of (the Constable as otherwise, that he hath used his best (Endeavour to Levy the said Sum on the Goods of the said (George Moule, but that no Sufficient Distress Could be (Found Wheron to Levy the Same.
Time Expired and was Discharged the 5th December 1788	(Ann Searle, a pauper of the poor House of Henham, Committed (15th November 1788, by William Campbell Clerk, to be Corrected and kept (to hard Labour for 21 days, being Convicted of refusing to (wear the Badge with a Large Roman P, together with the (first letter of the name of the said parish, Contrary to the Statute (in that Case made and provided
Discharged by the same Justice 10th January 1789	(Mary Watson, a pauper of the poor House of Henham, Committed (15th November 1788, by William Campbell Clerk, to be safely kept until (she should be Discharged by due Course of Law, being Convicted of (being a Rogue and Vagabond, for that she the said Mary (Watson having been before Convicted of being Idle and (without Employment, and of being a Lewd and Disorderly (woman.

Codicil to John Clifton's Will, 1783 (fig. 35)

A Codicil to be Added to and made part of the last Will / and Testament of me John Clifton of Oundle in the County of / Northampton, Joiner, which Will is Dated the 29th day of / January 1783. I Give and bequeath to my Sister Elizabeth Goodliff / All the Goods, Bed and Bedding as they now stand in the Chamber over / my parlour where I now live, Also All my Table linen and Bed linen of / All sorts in my Chests or Elsewhere All the Glass ware and Crockery in my corner / Cubboard, All my Earthenware of all sorts, half my glass Bottles, my 3 Gallon Stone / Bottle, my 4 gallon Barrell, two Brass cocks the Oak Dining Table in my house, / the old common Table and Buffet stool, my Jersy reel and horn lanthern / In the Parlour and pantry; My Chest Bed with the furniture to it as it stands / my Arm Chair that I usually sit in, and the low Brown chair and the old low / chair, the close stool chair and pewter pan, my Tea chest and six silver spoons / my box with my money Scales and weights, my other scales with all the Brass / and lead weights to them, my warming pan, my common Brass pot and Tea kettle / all the maps and pictures in my parlour that are framed, my little map of London / and the map of old London, either my large brass pot or great kettle (which she chuses) / my frying pan and little Gridiron, my chopper and Steelyards, my Box, Iron and / Smoothing Irons and rest, my Plumb tree round table and the little square table / the old Sconse and my Watch, my Tongs, poker and the rest of my fire utensils, pot hook / my Bucket and little tray cuttin, my knife tray with the knives and forks in it, . . . /

Overseer of the Poor's Accounts, 1747 (fig. 22)

The Disbursements of William Reed	£	s	d
Five days my self and horse to Alderchurch to apprehend Samuel Cocket by order of Jonathon Wyldbore Esquire	1	0	0
Paid Charges	1	5	10
Bringing Susan Fisher from Dogsthorpe to Peterborough 2 several days	''	3	''
Paid for their Marriage Charges	''	5	6
Paid to Mr. Strong for a Warrant to apprehend Samuel Cocket	''	2	''
My own time	''	2	''
Paid for the Charges of her lying in etc by order of Jonathon Wyldbore Esquire	1	2	6
Paid to ye Midwife for laying her	''	5	''
Paid to Charles Marsley for ye maintenance of Jane Curtis and a Nurse 5 days by order of ditto	''	8	''
Going to Stamford with Richard Toach to have his knee set and charges there	''	7	''
Paid for ye setting of his knee	''	2	10
Paid Richard Toach at same time	''	2	''
My own time	''	1	6
Paid Richard Toach by order of Jonathon Wyldbore Esquire 20 weeks collection from ye 18th of October to the 29th February	1	''	''
Paid him 4 weeks ditto to the 28th March	''	6	''
Paid him 4 weeks to the 25th April	''	8	''
Bringing Mrs. King's Goods to Peterborough	''	2	6
Paid for a Load of Turf for Widow Crading	''	11	''
Paid George Pank for a Load of Turf for Widow Taller	''	10	''
Carried over	8	4	8

Great and Little Chishill Enclosure Award, 1818 (fig. 27)

	And we the said Commissioners have set out and appointed and do hereby award and confirm the following
Public Roads	public carriage Roads and Highways and also the Following Bridle and Driftway and private roads through and over the lands and grounds by the said Act directed to be divided and allotted and also by and with the consents of the owners thereof through and over certain ancient Inclosures in the said parish of Great Chishill that is to say
Hayden Road	One public Carriage road and highway called the Hayden road of the breadth of thirty feet from the east end of the village of Great Chishill in its ancient course between Ayletts field and Down field until it passes between ancient inclosures in
Barley Road	the said parish of Great Chishill One other public carriage road and highway called the Barley road of the breadth of thirty feet from a lane or street near the church in the village of Great Chishill aforesaid in or near its ancient course between Great and Little Mudlins Dane Fields and over Mill field to a public road in the parish
The Barkway Road	of Barley One other public carriage road and highway called the Barkway road of the breadth of thirty feet from the end of White Horse lane in Great Chishill aforesaid in its ancient course by the Causeway bush to Sharpenhoe end lane in
Little Chishill Road	the said parish of Barley One other public Carriage road and highway called the Little Chishill road of the breadth of thirty feet branching out of the last described road at or near a Cottage and Orchard belonging to Joseph Wilkerson and proceeding in or

Christeninges 1676

Mark the sonne of Thomas Woodford and Margaret his wife was baptized December the third

Thomas the sonne of James Luckett and Elizabeth his wife was baptized December the fifth

Mark the sonne of Samuel and Anne Pace was baptized November the nineteenth

John the sonne of John Mabb and Susanna his wife was baptized December the eight

John the sonne of Thomas Willis and Jane his wife was baptised December the twelveth

Mariages 1676

James Barry was lawly married unto Margaret Essex November the thirtyeth

Henery Males was lawfully married unto Mary Moore December the seaventeenth

William Philip was lawfully married unto Elizabeth More December the seaven and twentyeth

Burialles 1676

Mary Serjant widow was buried December the twelveth

Anne the daughter of John and Margery Sparrow was buried January the fifth

Anne the wife of James Daniel of St. Clements parish was buried January the fifth

Anne the daughter of the widow Philip was buried January the eight

Anne Wright was buried January the nineth

A true and perfect Inventory of all and singular ye Goods and chattels of Robert Bee of Harmstone in ye County of Lincolne, Weaver, late deceased, Viewed, Valued, and Appraised this fourth day of February Anno Domini 1696 by us (whose Names are under written) in manner and form following. viz.

		£	s	d
Imprimis his Purse and Apparel		10	00	00
In the Hall				
Item Two Tables, one Form, 9 Chairs, one Pewter-Case with Pewter, and Brass, Fire-Irons, and other necessary things		4	00	00
In the Parlour				
Item One Cupboard, and Table, Three Chests and Linnens, one Long Settle, two Chaires, one stoole, a Clock and some other things		5	00	00
In his Book good and bad Debts		40	00	00
In the Buttery				
Item Two brass Pots, two Pans, some wearing Pewter one Table, Milk-Vessel, and other necessaries		1	10	00
In the Chamber over ye Parlour				
Item Two Bed-steads and Furniture thereun to belonging, One Table, one Chest, and bedding therein, and three Chairs		10	00	00
In the Chamber over the Hall				
Item Two Bed-steads and Bedding, three sacks of Pease one Wool-wheel, three Tow-wheels		3	10	00
In the Kitching and Cellar				
Item One Copper, and other Brewing-Vessel, several Barrels, one Wash-Tub, and other small Tubs and Pails, two Bacon-Flitches, a parcel of Coals, and several other small things		10	00	00
In ye Shop				
Item Three Weaving Looms, one Warping-Fat and Warping-Barrs, Gears, and all other Materials belonging to the shop		5	00	00
In ye out Chambers, Kiln, and Malt-house				
Item Malt and Barley 120 quarters		110	00	00
Item Forty quarters of Oats		18	00	00
Item Twelve strike of Oat meal		2	13	04
Item Several Sacks, two Hair-cloths, Measures, Shovels, and several other necessaries for ye Malt House, and Kiln		4	00	00
In the Yard and Field				
Item One Pease Stack		3	00	00
Item Rye Threshed		2	00	00
Item Corn sown, and Land Till'd		5	00	00
Item Two Stacks of Hay		10	00	00
Item Seven Cows four Yearlings, two Stears		25	00	00
Item and five Horses		15	00	00
Item Six Swine		9	00	00
Item Five Score Sheep, Stack-fences, and Cratches		33	06	08
Item Carts and Cart-gears, Plow and Plow-gears and all materials belonging to Husbandry		7	00	00
Item The Poultery		0	06	00
Item Things unseen and forgotton		0	4	06
The Total sum		333	10	06

John Clifton's Diary, 1779 (fig. 47)

(Left-hand page)
Boring and Jointing the old bottom pipe
into the New top piece

Saturday 18th Some rain to Day
My Self with my men

Mr. Truss and John Hill ¾ of a Day
setting the Pump Down — then wet

The Wells are very low all over the
town the weather has been so remarkably
Dry most part of the Summer

A Certain Man performed the following
most glorious Bolting match at a Gentlemans
house on Wednesday last for Dinner
first a fine Upheap plate of fish with a
    flowing Quantity of rich Sauce
next a large fishes Joll with Sauce
next a Beautiful large plate of Ham and fowl
next a heavenly large plate of Venison and Sauce
next another Ditto as fine as that
next a Glorious wedge of rich plum pudding
    And 6 fine horns of Ale to relish the whole

    No burial nor wedding this week

(Right-hand page)
    Thursday 23rd Statis Day
My Self sliving about
On the road just before my Door to night

a wooden piece of a Battle was fought
between Bob Sutton and a little fellow of
some where, but Hellion poll Haines and old
Betty Wright and Mother Munton being all
of the Dead Flesh sort, instantly siezed poor
Bob, and with staring flaming Eyes, and foaming
Chops and a hideous savage countenance they
Dragged him down the Entry backward and side
way and every way — — I can't Describe it
for want of room

    Friday 24th a finish Day
My Self about home
Old Mother Underwood possessed with
the Devil to night and wanted to Murder
old Tom White down Thunder -t Alley

    Saturday 25th a Fine Day — No events

    Burial but no wedding this week

Instructions to Constables to make Hue and Cry, 1697 (fig. 14)

    To all Constables or other officers
concerned for execution of these presents /
Whereas George Moody some what tall of
stature aged about 36 yeares with short /
Browne hair a Readish Beard in an old grey
hatt an old ffustian ffrock a Red / Stuff wast
Coat printed with Black and a paire of old
Teeking Breeches and was / Duble ffettered
as also William Hoot low of Stature aged
about 26 years with / bushy Browne Hair in
a Darke grey Coat a grey hatt and old
Leathern Breeches / and both of them
Roundish viisaged and Did both break out of
Cambridge Castle this / last night of the 3rd
Instant These are therefore in his Majesties
name strictly to / charge and comand you
and every of you forthwith upon sight
hereof to make Hue / and Cry after the said
George Moody and William Hoote as well on
horse Back as on foot / and if you can take
or apprehend them or either of them then to
carry him or them / before the next Justice
of the peace of any County or place where he
or they shall be / found to be dealt withall
according to Law and herein you are not to
faile but / to use your utmost Diligence as
youl answer the contrary at your perill dated
under / my hand and seale at Cambridge this
4th day of November anno domini / 1697
                    William Cooke
To goe North East
        J.A.

Petition from prisoners in the Essex gaol, 1674 (fig. 21)

The humble peticon of Richard Hals and all the prisners
in the Common County Gayle beinge nine
                in number
Humbly Sheweth
That one John Smyth committed theather for breach
of the peace, by the oath of his reputed wife, is by
his excessive breedinge of lice in amost foul and
lamantable Condition Stincks soe horridly and is soe
Full of vermine that all the prisners have bene strucke
downe and sicke by the noyseome stanch that comes from
him, And will in the end poysen them all
    May itt therefore please your good Honours
    to commisserate therie sad condition keept
    close upp in one rome with a deade Carkaise
    for noe deade man smells worse, then Smyth
    doth liveinge, And breeds vermine soe
    fast that they must of necessitie bee all
    eaten upp except releived by your Honours in
    setting Smyth att libertie

Churchwarden's Accounts, 1710 (fig. 13)

1710	Daniel Blackburn Churchwarden Disbursements	
April 13	Wood materialls and work to mend ye Church gate	0:0:11
	Paid for mending ye Church flagon	0:0:6
16	Bread and wine for ye Communion on Low Sonday	0:4:9
18	Visitation Charges at St. Martins	0:2:10
	Paid for 2 Double Stamps for Jonathen Kirchins Indentures	0:2:4
17	given to ye Ringers on the news of our forceing ye french Lines	0:1:0
5 May	To Mr. Edings man for a HedgHog	0:0:2
June 13	Earnest and Charges when we agreed with ye Painter to Draw ye Queen's Armes Pater Noster and Creed	0:1:8
14	Paid Jonathen Hanes for Surplis Mending and washing and wire for ye Clock	2:3
August 1	Paid for church Door Key mending and Irons to set up frames	0:3:3
4	Paid Adam Cook for a Badger Kil'd ith Steepings	0:1:0
26	To ye Ringers and most of ye Neighbours to Drink when we Rowted ye french forces in Spaine	0:7:0
September 8	Carriage of a Load of Stone and Lime from Ketton and Loading, and Tole at Stamford and Barnick	0:8:11
13	Carriage of an other Load, Loading Tole etc Drink	0:9:4
15	Paid Anthony Ashley for Stone Lime and work at Church Porch	2:2:0
	Diging and Carriage of Gravill and sand for Church Porch	0:1:6
22	Paid ffrancis Crowson for Laying Rough Paving and 3 Load of Sand and Gravill without Church Porch	0:2:2
October 3rd	Visitation Charges at St. Martins	0:6:3
23	Paid ye Apparator for a Proclamation for a ffast to be kept on ye 7 of November 1710 and a Book appointed for ye same	0:1:6
November 5	to ye Ringers as Usuall	0:5:0

Information given by Isaac Woods concerning the stealing of a length of cloth, 1788 (fig. 20)

Essex   The Information of Isaac Woods of Braintree
in the said County Bay Weaver taken upon Oath this 10th day of
November 1788 before one Nicholas Wakeham D.D. One of his
Majesty's Justices of the Peace in and for the said County
Who on his Oath saith That on Thursday night the 17th or Friday
morning the 18th of July last past, the Weaving Shop of him the said
Isaac Wood was broken open and about fifty yards of Bays the
property of Mr. Joseph Savill were cut from the Loom and feloniously
taken and carried away; and this Informant further saith That
he hath seen several Pieces of Bays which he hath been informed
were sold to divers Persons by one William Appleton late of
Braintree aforesaid Weaver, and that the said Pieces of Bays are part of
the Bays so cut and stolen from this Informant's Shop as aforesaid;
And this Informant further saith that between thirty and forty
Pounds of yarn the property of the said Joseph Savill were also
at the same Time feloniously stolen taken and Carried away from
the said Shop; and further saith That he hath probable cause
to suspect and doth Suspect that the said William Appleton and
One Benjamin Usher (not yet taken) were the Persons who broke open
the said Shop and feloniously took and carried away the said Bays
and Yarn as aforesaid

Sworn the Day and year first   The Mark of
above written before me   X
                                                  Isaac Woods.
    N. Wakeham

Glossary

---

archives historical records.

bond a binding agreement.

borough a town with privileges of self-government given by royal charter.

calendar list or register (of prisoners etc).

clerk secretary and administrator (parish clerk, clerk to the justices, etc).

constable elected officer with responsibility for local peacekeeping.

corporation the governing body of a borough.

diocese the church district administered by a bishop.

directory book giving information about an area and listing residents and tradesmen.

dole money or goods distributed from a charity.

enclosure the division of open fields or common land into privately-owned fields marked out by fences, etc.

engrossing hand formal handwriting style used for legal documents.

enumerator person responsible for counting and recording information at a census.

executor person appointed to carry out the instructions of a will.

glebe land belonging to a church which was farmed or rented out by the clergyman.

hue and cry system for raising the alarm and giving chase after a suspected criminal.

impropriator layman who had bought up the right to receive tithes.

incumbent clergyman attached to a particular church, and receiving the benefits which went with it.

indenture agreement (e.g. between apprentice and master) written in duplicate and cut apart along a wavy line.

indictment formal accusation charging someone with an offence.

inventory detailed list of possessions.

minutes summary recording the proceedings of a committee meeting.

nuisance minor infringement of the law.

overseer parish official with responsibility for the poor.

palaeography the study and interpretation of old writing.

parchment animal skins used for writing on.

parish an area with its own church and clergyman.

petty small or minor (e.g. petty sessions, petty constable).

probate the official proving of a will.

Quarter Sessions meetings of the Justices, held four times a year in each county.

secretary hand handwriting style used in the sixteenth and seventeenth centuries.

settlement the right to live permanently in a parish.

surveyor parish official responsible for the maintenance of the roads.

terrier list of property and land (e.g. belonging to the church in a particular parish).

tithe a tenth part of the produce of the land, to be given to the church.

transcript a written or printed copy of a document.

turnpike road which could be passed along only after payment of a toll.

vagrant a wanderer from place to place.

vellum fine parchment, traditionally made from calf skin.

vestry the body of parishioners who met to discuss parish business.

Date Chart

The period for which records were required to be kept and the period from which they have actually survived are often very different. Availability varies widely from one parish to another and from Record Office to Record Office. This chart provides a guide to the approximate period for which local records of different types are most likely to be found.

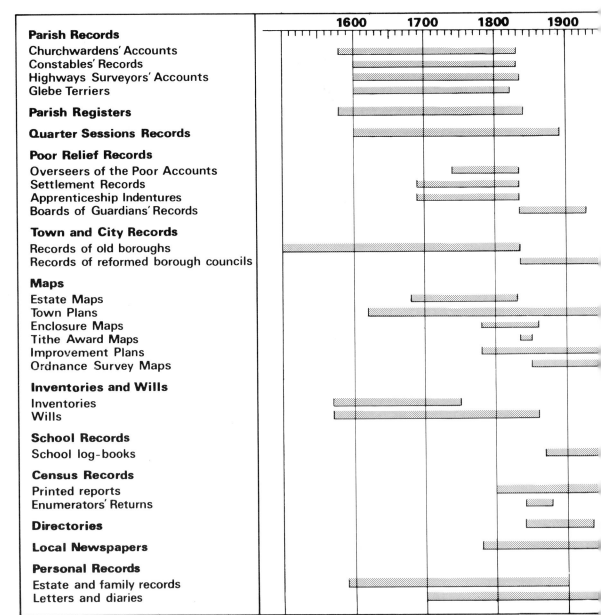

	1600	**1700**	**1800**	**1900**

Parish Records
Churchwardens' Accounts
Constables' Records
Highways Surveyors' Accounts
Glebe Terriers

Parish Registers

Quarter Sessions Records

Poor Relief Records
Overseers of the Poor Accounts
Settlement Records
Apprenticeship Indentures
Boards of Guardians' Records

Town and City Records
Records of old boroughs
Records of reformed borough councils

Maps
Estate Maps
Town Plans
Enclosure Maps
Tithe Award Maps
Improvement Plans
Ordnance Survey Maps

Inventories and Wills
Inventories
Wills

School Records
School log-books

Census Records
Printed reports
Enumerators' Returns

Directories

Local Newspapers

Personal Records
Estate and family records
Letters and diaries

List of Local Record Offices

This list gives the addresses of County and Borough Record Offices in England and Wales. Fuller details can be found in the booklet *Record Repositories in Great Britain*, produced by Her Majesty's Stationery Office. Most County Record Offices were set up before local government re-organization in 1974, and the records of parishes which changed counties can usually be found in the Record Office of the old county.

AVON
Bath City Record Office, Guildhall, Bath
Bristol Record Office, The Council House, College Green, Bristol

BEDFORDSHIRE
Bedfordshire Record Office, County Hall, Bedford

BERKSHIRE
Berkshire Record Office, Shire Hall, Shinfield Park, Reading

BUCKINGHAMSHIRE
Buckinghamshire Record Office, County Hall, Aylesbury

CAMBRIDGESHIRE
Cambridgeshire Record Office, Shire Hall, Castle Hill, Cambridge
Cambridgeshire Record Office, School Walk, Huntingdon

CHESHIRE
Cheshire Record Office, The Castle, Chester
Chester City Record Office, Town Hall, Chester

CLEVELAND
Cleveland County Libraries, Archives Department, 81 Borough Road, Middlesborough

CORNWALL
Cornwall Record Office, County Hall, Truro

CUMBRIA
Cumbria Record Office, The Castle, Carlisle
Cumbria Record Office, County Offices, Kendal
Cumbria Record Offices, 140 Duke Street, Barrow-in-Furness

DERBYSHIRE
Derbyshire Record Office, County Offices, Matlock

DEVON
Devon Record Office, Castle Street, Exeter
West Devon Area Record Office, Unit 3, Clare Place, Coxside, Plymouth

DORSET
Dorset Record Office, County Hall, Dorchester

DURHAM
Durham County Record Office, County Hall, Durham

ESSEX
Essex Record Office, County Hall, Chelmsford
Essex Record Office, Southend Branch, Central Library, Victoria Avenue, Southend-on-Sea

GLOUCESTERSHIRE
Gloucestershire Record Office, Worcester Street, Gloucester

HAMPSHIRE
Hampshire Record Office, 20 Southgate Street, Winchester
Portsmouth City Records Office, 3 Museum Road, Portsmouth
Southampton City Record Office, Civic Centre, Southampton

HEREFORD AND WORCESTER
Hereford and Worcester Record Office, County Buildings, St. Mary's Street, Worcester
Hereford Record Office, The Old Barracks, Harold Street, Hereford

HERTFORDSHIRE
Hertfordshire Record Office, County Hall, Hertford

HUMBERSIDE
Humberside County Record Office, County Hall, Beverley
South Humberside Area Record Office, Town Hall Square, Grimsby
Kingston upon Hull City Record Office, 79 Lowgate, Kingston upon Hull

KENT
Kent Archives Office, County Hall, Maidstone
Kent Archives Office, South East Kent Branch, Folkestone Central Library, Grace Hill, Folkestone
Canterbury Cathedral Archives and City and Diocesan Record Office, The Precincts, Canterbury

LANCASHIRE
Lancashire Record Office, Bow Lane, Preston

LEICESTERSHIRE
Leicestershire Record Office, 57 New Walk, Leicester

LINCOLNSHIRE
Lincolnshire Archives Office, The Castle, Lincoln

GREATER LONDON
Greater London Record Office, The County Hall, London
Corporation of London Records Office, PO Box 270, Guildhall, London
Westminster City Libraries, Archives Department,

Victoria Library, 160 Buckingham Palace Road, London
(Collections of local records are held by many other London borough libraries)

GREATER MANCHESTER
Greater Manchester Record Office, County Hall, Piccadilly Gardens, Manchester
Manchester City Archives Department, Central Library, St. Peter's Square, Manchester
Bolton Metropolitan Borough Archives, Civic Centre, Le Mans Crescent, Bolton
Wigan Record Office, Town Hall, Leigh
Salford Archives Centre, 658/662 Liverpool Road, Irlam, Manchester

MERSEYSIDE
Merseyside County Archives, 64-66 Islington, Liverpool
Liverpool Record Office, City Libraries, William Brown Street, Liverpool
Wirral Archives, Birkenhead Reference Library, Borough Road, Birkenhead

WEST MIDLANDS
Birmingham Reference Library, Chamberlain Square, Birmingham
Coventry City Record Office, Room 220, Broadgate House, Broadgate, Coventry
Dudley Archives and Local History Department, Central Library, 3 St. James's Road, Dudley
Walsall Archives Service, Central Library, Lichfield Street, Walsall
Wolverhampton Borough Archives, Central Library, Snow Hill, Wolverhampton

NORFOLK
Norfolk Record Office, Central Library, Norwich

NORTHAMPTONSHIRE
Northamptonshire Record Office, Delapré Abbey, Northampton

NORTHUMBERLAND
Northumberland Record Office, Melton Park, North Gosforth, Newcastle

NOTTINGHAMSHIRE
Nottinghamshire Record Office, County House, High Pavement, Nottingham

OXFORDSHIRE
Oxfordshire County Record Office, County Hall, Oxford

SHROPSHIRE
Shropshire Record Office, Shirehall, Abbey Foregate, Shrewsbury

SOMERSET
Somerset Record Office, Obridge Road, Taunton

STAFFORDSHIRE
Staffordshire Record Office, County Buildings, Eastgate Street, Stafford
Lichfield Joint Record Office, Lichfield Library, Bird Street, Lichfield

SUFFOLK
Suffolk Record Office, Ipswich Branch, County Hall, Ipswich
Suffolk Record Office, Bury St. Edmunds Branch, School Hall Street, Bury St. Edmunds

SURREY
Surrey Record Office, County Hall, Penrhyn Road, Kingston upon Thames
Surrey Record Office, Guildford Muniment Room, Castle Arch, Guildford

EAST SUSSEX
East Sussex Record Office, Pelham House, St. Andrews Lane, Lewes

WEST SUSSEX
West Sussex Record Office, County Hall, West Street, Chichester

TYNE AND WEAR
Tyne and Wear Archives Department, Blandford House, West Blandford Street, Newcastle upon Tyne
Tyne and Wear Archives Department, Local Studies Centre, Howard Street, North Shields
Gateshead Central Library, Prince Consort Road, Gateshead

WARWICKSHIRE
Warwick County Record Office, Priory Park, Cape Road, Warwick

ISLE OF WIGHT
Isle of Wight County Record Office, 26 Hillside, Newport

WILTSHIRE
Wiltshire Record Office, County Hall, Trowbridge

NORTH YORKSHIRE
North Yorkshire County Record Office, County Hall, Northallerton
York Archives, Art Gallery Building, Exhibition Square, York
Borthwick Institute, York University, St. Anthony's Hall, Peasholme Green, York

SOUTH YORKSHIRE
South Yorkshire County Record Office, Cultural Activities Centre, Ellin Street, Sheffield
Sheffield City Library, Archives Division, Central Library, Surrey Street, Sheffield
Doncaster Archives Department, Bentley Library, Cooke Street, Bentley, Doncaster
Rotherham Metropolitan Borough, Brian O'Malley Central Library, Walker Place, Rotherham

WEST YORKSHIRE
West Yorkshire Record Office, Registry of Deeds, Newstead Road, Wakefield
Bradford Archives Department, Central Library, Prince's Way, Bradford
Calderdale Metropolitan Borough Archives Department, Central Library, Lister Lane, Halifax
Leeds Archives Department, Chapeltown, Sheepscar, Leeds

Kirklees Libraries and Museums Service, Princess
    Alexandra Walk, Huddersfield
Wakefield Department of Archives and Local Studies,
    Library Headquarters, Balne Lane, Wakefield
WALES
CLWYD
Clwyd Record Office, Hawarden Branch, The Old
    Rectory, Hawarden, Deeside
Clwyd Record Office, Ruthin Branch, 46 Clwyd
    Street, Ruthin

DYFED
Dyfed Archive Service, County Hall, Carmarthen
Cardiganshire Area Record Office, County Office,
    Marine Terrace, Aberystwyth
Carmarthenshire Area Record Office, County Hall,
    Carmarthen
Pembrokeshire Area Record Office, The Castle,
    Haverfordwest

SOUTH GLAMORGAN
Glamorgan Archive Service, Glamorgan Record
    Office, County Hall, Cathays Park, Cardiff
(serves Mid, South and West Glamorgan)
GWENT
Gwent County Record Office, County Hall,
    Cwmbran

GWYNEDD
Gwynedd Archives Service, Caernarfon Area Record
    Office, County Offices, Shire Hall Street,
    Caernarfon
Gwynedd Archives Service, Dolgellau Area Record
    Office, Cae Penarlag, Dolgellau
Gwynedd Archives Service, Anglesey Area Record
    Office, Shire Hall, Llangefni

Books for Further Reading

F.G. Emmison,
Archives and Local History,
Methuen, 1978

F.G. Emmison and Irvine Gray,
County Records,
Historical Association Pamphlet, 1973

F.G. Emmison,
How to Read Local Archives,
Historical Association Pamphlet, 1967

David Iredale,
Discovering Local History,
Shire Publications, 1977

David Iredale,
Enjoying Archives,
David and Charles, 1973

Michael Morgan,
Historical Sources in Geography,
Butterworth, 1979

Rowland Parker,
The Common Stream,
Paladin, 1976

John Richardson,
The Local Historian's Encyclopedia,
Historical Publications, 1981

W.E. Tate,
The Parish Chest,
Cambridge University Press, 1969

John West,
Village Records,
Macmillan, 1982

Index

The numbers in **bold type** refer to the figure numbers of the illustrations